GREGORIAN CHANTS

An Illustrated History of Religious Chanting

Colin R. Shearing

Published in 2004 by Mercury Books
20 Bloomsbury Street
London WC1B 3JH

© 2004 Mercury Books

Designed and produced for Mercury Books
by Open Door Limited
Langham, Rutland
Editing: Stephen Chumbley and Mary Morton

Title: Gregorian Chants
ISBN: 1 904668 52 6

Images supplied by:
AKG-Images, London: pages 10, 12, 16, 18, 21, 22-23, 25, 27, 29,
31, 33, 35, 37, 38, 39, 40, 43, 44, 47, 51, 53, 57, 59, 60-61, 64,
68, 71, 73, 74, 76, 78, 80-81, 83, 86-87, 88, 90, 93, 95, 101, 113,
115, 123, 124, 126, 135, 136, 137, 138
Corbis: pages 3, 6, 7, 8-9, 11, 67, 120, 121, 128

GREGORIAN CHANTS

An Illustrated History of Religious Chanting

Colin R. Shearing

MERCURY BOOKS

Contents

 # Contents

 # Introduction

Chanting is unaccompanied sung melody, rhythms and melodic contours, which are closely tied to the spoken rhythms and inflections of various texts. These texts can either be sacred or secular but the term chanting usually refers to sacred liturgical music.

Chanting has been used in religious ceremonies since mankind first learnt to vocalise. All ancient peoples have used chanting as a way of altering consciousness and putting themselves in touch with the Divine. The Ancient Egyptians depicted choirs and instrumentalists on their tombs and Eastern Orthodox Christianity today uses similar chants in its religious ceremonies. The early Greeks considered music to be of mathematical and cosmic significance and discovered the frequency proportions that defined the intervals that we hear today.

An initial from Pius II's Book of Psalms annotated in Gregorian chant. It comes from the Orvieto cathedral and several painters were commissioned to illuminate it. The scene depicts the adoration of the shepherds.

In India chants are called mantras and the Hindus chant daily from their holy books, each particular Hindu god having his or her particular mantra or chant. Indian chant is reputed to raise the consciousness of the chanter in tune with the particular deity being invoked. The most famous of these mantras is the use of the word 'Om'. Throughout the East, chanting is used by Buddhists, both Mahayana and Zen, as well as in the Japanese Shinto religion and by Mongolian shamans with their overtone chants.

Present-day chanting in the Western world takes its repertoire from Jewish liturgical chant, called cantillation. The Jewish reading of the scriptures by cantillation was and is a great feature of synagogue worship. The early Christian church took not only its modes and scales but also melodies from the ancient Hebrews. Many of the texts in Christian chants are taken from or based upon the Psalms of David, an Old Testament book shared by both Jews and Christians. The chant used in the Roman Catholic Mass today

is an evolution of the chant that Jesus would have heard in the Temple and the synagogues of his day. Other types of Christian chant, often called Plainsong, were developed during the first millennium of the Christian era. In Milan, a repertory called Ambrosian was developed, named after St Ambrose, which is still used in some Roman Catholic services in Milan. Until about the eleventh century, there was a chant repertory called Mozarabic, named after the Mozarab Christians who lived in Islamic Spain during the Middle Ages, and this chant still survives today in a few Spanish cathedrals. Within the Islamic tradition, there are chants using the ninety-nine names of Allah, called 'the beautiful names'. Up until the ninth century, France had its own chant repertory called Gallican. The flowering of the chant was reached in the early seventh century after Pope Gregory the Great had made a collection of Roman chants and assigned them specific places within the liturgy. These are known as Gregorian chants and there are over 3,000 different Gregorian chants extant today. The Eastern Christian churches developed their own style of chanting, many of which are still used; Armenian, Byzantine, Russian, Greek and Syrian repertories being the most important. Many of these have been incorporated into the Gregorian repertory. In the Protestant churches only the Church of England encouraged the extensive use of chanting and has a repertory called Anglican chant.

Portrait of Pope Gregory I.
He was the author of dialogues,
known especially for The Moralia
(Morals from the Book of Job).
He was canonized by popular
acclaim.

Choral music itself is written for choruses or choirs and the religious chant developed out of the secular chanting of folk songs within tribal cultures. This chanting usually accompanied manual labour. Among the world's many choral traditions are the polyphonic, polyrhythmic choruses of Africa, the relaxed harmonies of the Slavic areas of Europe, the tense-voiced women's canons of the Balkans, the unison choral singing of Indonesian gamelan orchestras, the unison and polyphonic choruses of Oceania (New Zealand, Fiji and Tonga), the Native American Navaho healing chants and the New Age culture is currently developing a new repertory of chants to incorporate within their own eclectic spiritual beliefs.

Notes on dates

The term CE for 'Common Era' has been used in this book rather than AD (Anno Domini – in the Year of our Lord) and BCE for 'Before Common Era' rather than BC (Before Christ) to reflect the wide number of different beliefs of the readers.

An initial from Pius II's Book of Psalms annotated in Gregorian chant. It comes from the Orvieto cathedral and several painters were commissioned to illuminated it. One initial depicts the Virgin Mary holding the Christ child surrounded by saints. The second initial depicts Christ being baptised by John the Baptist in a river. The Holy Spirit is represented by the dove.

'Homage to thee, O thou glorious Being, thou who art dowered with all sovereignty. O Tum-Heru-Khuti when thou risest in the horizon of heaven a cry of joy goeth forth to thee from all people.'

(From the 'Hymn to Ra')

Gregorian chant, as a feature of Christian worship, has been around for many centuries in the form it takes today. However, the chanting from which it is derived is much older and by delving back into the ancient cultures which were the foundation of Christianity we can see its early origins and learn how it evolved.

CHANTING IN ANCIENT EGYPT

In Ancient Egypt, the God Osiris was considered the god of music. In the temples, choral groups were formed to praise the god. The God Horus, son of Osiris, was known as the god of harmony and order.

Painting of Osiris – the God of Music, in the tomb of Horemheb, Thebes. In this depiction Osiris has green skin, a symbol of the renewal of life in Spring.

During the time of the New Kingdom, the 18th Dynasty, 1352–1069 BCE, the voice was given greater importance and emphasis in temple ritual. The human voice was considered as the transmitter of spirit and the purest and most honest expression of piety. During this time the God Tahuti named 'Osiris – True of Voice' had a particularly important ritual performed in the temples in honour of him. This was called 'The Release of Voice'. The Egyptians believed that the voice had magical powers. This was echoed by the Hebrews in their depiction of Creation, when it is said 'In the Beginning was the Word'. This Biblical story of Creation was taken and adapted from the Egyptian story of Creation.

By studying Egyptian frescoes it has been discovered that Egyptian music was generally calm and of a spiritual nature. It was only performed by priests; musicians and choristers always wore priests' clothing. Many Egyptian tombs depict choirs and instrumentalists, giving praise to both the Pharaoh and to their deities. In the 1950s (CE) an archaeological dig uncovered a set of clay tablets near the village of Ras Shamra in Syria. The tablets in the ancient Hurrian language date back to 1400 BCE and contain a hymn to the Moon God's wife Nikal, the Sun Goddess. These tablets contain detailed instructions for a singer, accompanied by a harpist, as well as instructions on how to tune the harp. Musicologists have been able to reproduce this hymn which is performed in harmony with thirds, sixths, fourths and fifths. This rare example also shows that polyphony was known in ancient music, centuries before it is believed to have been invented.

Horus – God of Harmony and Order, painted in the tomb of Horemheb, Thebes.

Perhaps the most famous hymns of Egypt are known as the 'Hymn to Ra' and the 'Hymn to Aten' composed by Akhenaten. Other well-known hymns are the 'Hymn to Hapy', which was used in worship to ensure the flooding of the Nile, and 'The Song of the Blind Harper'. The Egyptian Book of the Coming Forth By Day, known as the Egyptian Book of the Dead, also features a number of chants.

'At daybreak, when thou arisest on the horizon,
When thou shinest as the Aten by day,
Thou drivest away the darkness
and givest thy rays.'
(Hymn to Aten)

'Lightmaker who comes out of darkness,
Fattener of herds'
(Hymn to Hapy)

The Coptic Christian Church of present-day Egypt has preserved many of these chants and hymns in the original language of ancient Egypt and they are still used in their liturgy to the present day.

Egyptian, stelophore statue of Amenemope II (1479–1397 BC), with a hymn to the sun. Found at Dayr al-Madinah, Thebes in the Tomb of Amenemope.

Limestone, painted, height 55 cm.

CHANTING IN ISRAEL

> *'Let us sing a joyful song unto the Lord.'*
> *(Psalm 95)*

During the Israelites' sojourn in Egypt, they were greatly affected by the rituals, ceremonies and music of the Egyptians. When Moses led them out of Egypt, in approximately 1400 BCE, they took these traditions with them and translated them into their own language to form a greater part of their own religious liturgy. There are even scholars today who suggest that Akhenaten, who founded the first monotheistic religion of Egypt, was in fact the Moses of the Old Testament himself. The Hebrews' escape from the Egyptians is celebrated in the vividly descriptive 'Song of Moses' sung by the Children of Israel to the accompaniment of Miriam's dancing and timbrel (a hand drum) playing on the shores of the Red Sea.

Throughout the ancient history of the Jewish people, music and singing is mentioned with a frequency far exceeding its mention in the cultural history of any other people. In ancient texts such as the Old Testament and Talmud every event of popular rejoicing, such as a coronation or royal marriage, is accompanied by singers and musicians. The Company of the Prophets march together to the sound of a psaltery, a pipe and a harp and it is to the playing of a minstrel that the hand of the Lord comes upon Elisha so that the future becomes clear to his eyes. In the Old Testament when the Ten Tribes that revolted and formed the Kingdom of Israel disappeared under Assyrian captivity, nevermore to find their way back to the pages of history, the two remaining Tribes that formed the Kingdom of Judah still retain their love of singing, music and dance. It is only under Babylonian captivity in which their grief is so strong that their love of singing and music ceased.

> *'We hanged our harps upon the willows in the midst thereof. How shall we sing the Lord's song in a strange land?'*
> *(Psalm 137:1)*

When the tribes returned and the rebuilding of the Temple of Jerusalem was undertaken, the singers were restored to the functions their forefathers had exercised and at the laying of the foundations it is recorded 'the

priests in their apparel with trumpets, and the Levites, the sons of Asaph with cymbals, to praise the Lord after the ordinance of David the King of Israel, and they sang together by course in praising and giving thanks unto the Lord' (Ezra, Chapter 3).

During the reign of King David, out of 38,000 of the tribe of Levi, 4,000 were appointed as temple musicians and choristers. Every village in Israel had its own synagogue. The synagogue ritual was laid down officially after the destruction of Jerusalem and the Temple in 70 CE. The vocal part of the Jewish musical tradition was developed when the Jews migrated all across the Roman Empire. However, because of this diaspora there is an absence of instrumental music in the synagogues. This instrumental silence serves as a reminder that the glories of the temple worship of the past will someday be renewed. Psalms were sung during religious ceremonies in either call-and-response mode, that is the soloist followed by congregation, or antiphonally, that is one group followed by another.

Wind, string and percussion instruments are mentioned in the Old Testament but the only traditional Jewish instrument still used in ceremonies today is the Shofar, a primitive trumpet made from rams' horn. In some of the Old Testament scrolls, there are small markings above the text of the Psalms that is a system of musical notation called 'Ta'amim'. This system of marking the text with symbols is very similar to the earlier systems of notation used in Christian Plain chant.

The reading of the Scriptures by cantillation was and is a great feature of synagogue worship. Those books which are obligatory to read publicly had traditional tunes and it is very likely that when Jesus went into the synagogue and publicly read the Prophesies of Isiah, he used cantillation. The singing of the Book of Esther offers an example to accumulate popular tunes of the peoples amongst whom the Jews lived, by incorporating them in their synagogual cantillation so that they became part of the tradition. This cantillation or chanting was the duty of the Chazzan of a synagogue who needed to have a tenor or baritone voice and the ability to use it effectively, as well as a large repertory of traditional chants. These Chazzans, who acted as caretakers to the synagogues and also as keepers of the Torah scrolls, held a high status in the community. During the times of persecution, particularly in the Middle Ages, many of the 'Chazzanim' adopted a wandering life, becoming minstrels, and travelled from one Jewish community to another to seek their livelihood. Many adopted the Latin

term 'Cantor' over Chazzan to hide their Jewish identities and both terms continue to be used to this day.

The traditional cantillations for the reading of the 'Law' have to be memorised and there is a great deal of resemblance between Jewish cantillation and Christian Plainsong and in fact there are passages common to both. Cantillation is also used in the Jewish home on the first two nights of Passover, when the story of the redemption from Egypt is sung from the book Haggadah, by the master of the house. The Psalms of David, having been translated from Hebrew into Latin and English, form the greater body of the Christian liturgy used in chanting today.

'Sing to the LORD a new song;
sing to the LORD, all the earth.
Sing to the LORD, praise his name;
proclaim his salvation day after day.
Declare his glory among the nations,
his marvellous deeds among all peoples.
For great is the LORD and most worthy of praise;
he is to be feared above all gods.

For all the gods of the nations are idols,
but the LORD made the heavens.
Splendour and majesty are before him;
strength and glory are in his sanctuary.
Ascribe to the LORD, O families of nations,
ascribe to the LORD glory and strength.
Ascribe to the LORD the glory due his name;
bring an offering and come into his courts.
Worship the LORD in the splendour of his holiness;
tremble before him, all the earth.
Say among the nations, 'The LORD reigns.'
The world is firmly established, it cannot be moved;
he will judge the peoples with equity.
Let the heavens rejoice, let the earth be glad;
let the sea resound, and all that is in it;
let the fields be jubilant, and everything in them.
Then all the trees of the forest will sing for joy;
they will sing before the LORD, for he comes,
he comes to judge the earth.
He will judge the world in righteousness
and the peoples in his truth.'

(Psalm 96)

CHANTING IN ANCIENT GREECE

The Ancient Greeks considered music to be of mathematical and cosmic significance. Pythagoras of Samos, circa 500 BCE, discovered the frequency proportions that defined the musical intervals that we hear today. Pythagorian philosophers believed that these ratios also governed the movement of celestial bodies and other cosmic matters. Thus music came to be revered as the highest of intellectual and artistic pursuits. Ptolemy's treatise 'Harmonics' is the best extant reference on Ancient Greek musical theory. The Greeks used a system of modes known as 'tonoi', similar to present-day musical scales.

It is widely believed that Ancient Greek music was monophonic (melody only) or heterophonic (many instruments simultaneously playing different versions of the same melody). There are many literary references in Greek culture that describe the role of music and its effects on human behaviour. Ancient Greek music was an integrated part of other art forms, particularly dance, drama and poetry. The 'Iliad' and the 'Odyssey' by Homer are epic poems that were chanted as odes to the accompaniment of plucked string instruments. Because of this integration, Greek philosophers considered music and singing to have supernatural effects and that different types of music would affect human behaviour in different ways. For example, music or chanting in the Dorian mode would cause persons to become meditative, whereas music in the Phrygian mode would cause persons to become passionate and belligerent.

Pythagoras during sound experiments.

From 'Theoria Musicae', Venice 1492.

Woodcut, colour applied later.

THE RISE OF THE ROMAN CHURCH

The prevailing religion of Imperial Rome was polytheistic and had originated from the worship of nature. As Rome grew to statehood, the Gods of her neighbours had been incorporated into the religion, including Jupiter the Sky God and Mars the War God. Greek cults were also embraced and from 204 BCE the orgies of Cybele, the Asiatic Earth Goddess, and the hedonistic rituals of Dionysus Bacchus, the god of wine, were evident. As the Roman Empire spread eastwards, the Egyptian religion of Isis, the Universal Mother, was introduced, along with the Persian god Mithras. Eventually the Syrian solar religion of Sol Invictus (the unconquerable sun) became their all-encompassing belief. This cult had the sun as the ultimate giver of life and enabled all other cults to be included within it, with the Emperor as the earthly incarnation of the godhead.

In 66 CE the historian Flavius Josephus (37–100 CE), who was in fact a Hasmonaean Jew, had been appointed commander in the defence of Galilee. He had previously trained for the Pharisee priesthood but took military service when the Jews rose up against their Roman overlords. He subsequently became the foremost historian of that time and his writings, 'The Wars of the Jews' and 'The Antiquities of the Jews', provide great insight into the complex history of the Jews. He locates Jesus firmly within the historical framework of the time with no mention of his divinity, a concept which was to come later. Josephus wrote in around 80 CE when he was in Rome under the protection of the Emperor Vespasian. The Gospel of Mark which was to form part of the New Testament had been written a few years before. Gospel writings of that time were not anti-Roman, indeed the early Christians were more inclined to blame other Jews rather than Pilate for their persecution and because of the Jewish uprising of 66–70 CE which had failed, the newly emerging Christian cult believed that God had switched allegiance from the Jews to themselves. However, the position of these early Christians within the expanding Roman Empire was very precarious and often brought great danger. They were a small minority group with no legal status and from the time of Nero's crucifixion of Peter to the Edict of Milan in 313 CE (where Christianity was legally recognised) there were no fewer than thirty appointed Christian Bishops of Rome, the first of which, installed during Peter's lifetime by Paul in 58 CE, was the son of the British king Caractacus, known as Linus. By about 120 CE clerical appointments were made by group election and the candidates had to be citizens of Rome. There was also little or no connection between these Pauline Christians and the Jewish

Hadrian, Publius Aelius Hadrianus, Roman Emperor (117–38 CE); 76–138 CE. 'Hadrian and Antinous'. (Antinous, favourite of the Emperor; deified after his death in 130 CE by the latter).

Etching by G. Mochetti after a drawing by Bartolomeo Pinelli (1781–1835). From the series: Istoria Romana (1810).

Nazarene followers of Jesus and James the Just's own Judaic form. These heretical Jews settled mainly in Mesopotamia, Syria, southern Turkey and Egypt, as well as Britain and Gaul. These Judaic Christians culminated in the Eastern Orthodox Christian faith and the Paulines culminated in the Roman Catholic faith.

The Christians of Rome were suppressed because they challenged the traditional divinity of the Emperors. By the middle of the second century CE the original Nazarenes of Jesus' family were even more unpopular, not only with the Roman authorities but with the Pauline Christians, particularly Irenaeus, Bishop of Lyon, who condemned them as heretics for claiming that Jesus was a man and not of divine origin. In 135 CE, Jerusalem was again crushed by Roman legions under Emperor Hadrian and the surviving Jews were scattered from their homeland. Having reached the height of its glory in Hadrian's era (117–138 CE), Roman imperialism began to decline under Emperor Commodus and throughout the third century internal disputes left the borders of the Empire open to attack. In 235 CE, Emperor Maximus declared that all Christian bishops and priests should be arrested, their wealth confiscated and their churches burned. By the time of the Emperor Decius (249 CE) the Christians had become so rebellious that they were proclaimed criminals and a mass persecution began which continued into the reign of Diocletian who became Emperor in 284 CE (reigning until 305 CE). Diocletian removed all vestiges of democratic procedures and instituted an absolute monarchy. The Christians were required to offer sacrifices to him as god and suffered punishment for any disobedience. All churches were demolished and disciples were put to death. All books and testaments were publicly burned; all prominent Christians were barred from public office and Christian slaves were denied any hope of freedom. The protection of Roman law was withdrawn from them completely.

In order to counteract the persistent incursions into the Roman Empire by barbarian invaders, Diocletian established two separate units of power. The Western Empire was managed from Gaul and the Eastern Empire was centred at Byzantium. Galerius, the Governor of the Eastern Province, ruthlessly persecuted the Christians in his area but just before his death in 311 CE he surprisingly issued a decree of relaxation which gave the Christians the right of assembly. In 312 CE Constantine, who was born in England to an English mother, ruled jointly as Emperor in the West with Licinius as Emperor in the East. Notwithstanding its persecution, Christianity had increased its following considerably and was flourishing

in all corners of the Empire. Strangely, Christian evangelists were having more success in pacifying the barbarians than were the legions of Rome. Constantine, who was aware of the power of Christianity through his British family and realising that the Empire was beginning to fall apart, perceived Christianity as a unifying force that he could use to his own advantage. At the Battle of Milvian Bridge he announced that he had seen a vision of a cross in the sky accompanied by the words 'In hoc signo vinces' ('In this sign conquer'). The Christian bishops of the time were most impressed that a Roman Emperor had ridden to victory under their own banner. Constantine was to change the structure of Christianity for all time. 'In the future, we as the Apostle of Christ, will help choose the Bishop of Rome'. Quite suddenly Christianity became respectable and was approved as The Imperial Religion. Constantine subsequently became Caesar of all the Roman Empire in 324 CE and was known thereafter as Constantine the Great. Constantine, in breach of traditional practice, chose his own candidate to be the first imperial bishop who was crowned with great pomp and ceremony.

Apart from various cult beliefs the Romans had worshipped the Emperors in their capacity as gods descended from other gods. At the Council of Arles in 314 CE, Constantine had retained his own divine status by introducing the omnipotent god of the Christians as his personal sponsor. He then dealt with the anomalies of doctrine by replacing parts of the Christian ritual with the familiar and pagan traditions of Sol Invictus, mixed with Mithraism. In short the new religion of the Roman church was constructed as a hybrid to appease all influential factions. By this means Constantine ensured a common, unified world religion with himself at its head, to be known as the Roman Catholic Church.

'Praise the LORD.
Praise, O servants of the Lord,
praise the name of the Lord.
Let the name of the Lord be praised,
both now and forevermore.
From the rising of the sun to the place where it sets,
the name of the Lord is to be praised.'
(Psalm 113)

Constantine I, the Great, Roman-Byzant. emperor; c. 280–337 CE 'Constantine and the Labarum' (standard bearing the monogram of Christ used by Constantine in the battle of the Milvian Bridge 312 CE). Tapestry, Paris manufacture, after sketch, 1622, by Peter Paul Rubens (1577–1640) 'History of Constantine the Great'.

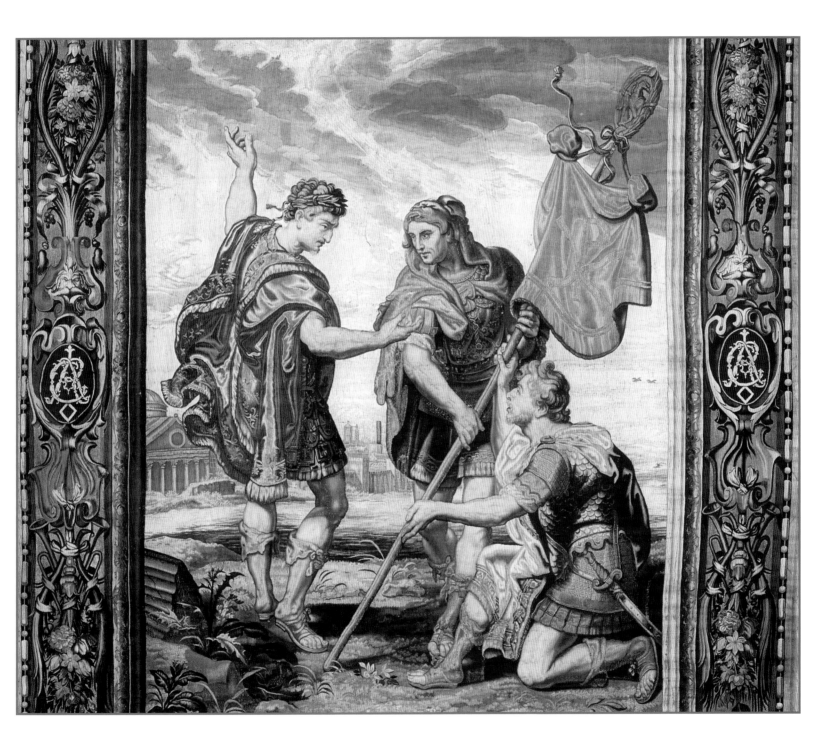

Halle (Saxony-Anhalt), Main University Building, Staircase.
'Theology: Paul preaching in Athens (Apostles 17, 22–23).'
Fresco, 1883/88, by Gustav Adolph Spangenberg (1828–1891).
From a cycle 'The Four Faculties'

 # The Golden Age
of the Christian Chant (300–800 CE)

> 'In principio erat Verbum et Verbum erat apud Deum et Deus erat Verbum.'
> 'In the beginning was the Word: and the Word was with God: and the Word was God.'
>
> (John 1:1)

THE DEVELOPMENT OF THE EARLY CHRISTIAN CHURCH

The early Christian Church came into being as a liturgical institution because the early Christians were Jews and Jewish worship was liturgical. The New Testament records many instances of liturgical worship, ranging from the purely Jewish practices of going into the temple to pray, to the Christian liturgy of the Rite of the Eucharist. The early Christian disciples did not in themselves create any new practices of worship any more than did their leader Jesus or the subsequent leader of the Nazarene sect, James the Just, Jesus' brother. They all prayed as Jews and worshipped as Jews. Early Christianity was regarded as a heretical branch of Judaism that itself split into two separate branches: one branch following the teachings of Paul, which culminated in the Roman Catholic Church, and the other adhering more closely to the Jewish forms of worship which followed a line of Apostolic teachers beginning with James the Just. This line culminated in the Celtic church which spread throughout the British Isles and Gaul and continues in the Eastern Orthodox Church.

From the contents of the many books written about early Christianity, it could easily be assumed that the Roman Church was the only true church of Jesus, whereas other Christ-related beliefs were false. This is far from the truth; many branches of Christianity were less pagan than that of the politically-contrived Church of Rome. These so-called heretical sects despised the idols and opulence of the Roman ideal and many were accordingly condemned themselves as being heathen and pagan by the Roman Church. In 318 CE, a spokesman of the Nazarene tradition of Jesus' family called Joses, who was a descendant of Jesus' brother Jude, journeyed to Rome to argue that the Christian church should really be

Constantine transferring the Imperial symbols of power, Phrygium and Baldachin, as well as the Lateran Palace to Pope Silvester I.

Fresco, 1246. Rome, Oratorio di S. Silvestro.

centred in Jerusalem, not in Rome and that the Bishop of Jerusalem should be of the hereditary bloodline of the Kings of the Jews, as was Jesus. Not surprisingly his demands were ignored. The original teachings had been superseded by a doctrine that was more amenable to the Imperial requirements of Constantine. Silvester, the Bishop of Rome at the time, even told this delegation that the power of salvation rested no longer in Jesus but in the Emperor Constantine. Shortly after this, at the Council of Nicaea, this threat to the Roman church was dealt with very expediently. The Pauline Christians had been expecting a second coming of their Messiah and Constantine needed to demolish this notion. The original mission of Jesus to free the Jews from Roman domination had failed because of the disunity amongst the Jews themselves. Constantine took advantage of this by implying that since it was he, the Emperor, who had ensured the Christians' freedom and safety within the Empire, then he was their true saviour, not Jesus. He knew of course that Jesus had been venerated as the son of God and this concept had to be demolished as well. At Nicaea, God was formally defined as three persons in one: a deity comprising three co-equal and co-eternal parts – the Father, the Son and the Holy Ghost. This was set out in the Nicene Creed which became part of the newly-forming Christian liturgy.

The Nicene Creed

'We believe in one God, the Father, the Almighty,
maker of heaven and earth,
of all that is, seen and unseen.

We believe in one Lord, Jesus Christ,
the only Son of God,
eternally begotten of the Father,
God from God, Light from Light,
true God from True God,
begotten not made, of One Being with the Father.
Through him all things were made.
For us and for our salvation
He came down from heaven: by the power
of the Holy Spirit
He became incarnate from the Virgin Mary,
and was made man.
For our sake he was crucified under Pontius Pilate;
He suffered death and was buried.
On the third day he rose again in accordance
with the Scriptures;
He ascended into heaven and is stead
at the right hand of the Father.
He will come again in glory to judge the living and the dead,
And his kingdom will have no end.

We believe in the Holy Spirit, the Lord, the giver of life,
Who proceeds from the Father and the Son,
With the Father and the Son he is worshipped and glorified.
He has spoken through the Prophets.
We believe in one holy catholic and apostolic Church.
We acknowledge one baptism for the forgiveness of sins.
We look for the resurrection of the dead, and the life of
the world to come.
Amen'

At this time, having bypassed the Jewish Jesus, the Messianic godhead became the Emperor Constantine and would have continued as such for his successors. In fact, once the historical Jesus had been sidelined, the Christian religion was said to have been named after a man called Crestus. Once Constantine had proclaimed himself God's Apostle on Earth, it then became his right to ratify appointments within the Church. In 330 CE, Constantine declared Byzantium the capital of the Eastern Roman Empire and renamed it Constantinople (what is now Istanbul in Turkey). The following year he convened a general council in Constantinople to further ratify the decisions of the Council of Nicaea. Once this form of Roman Christianity had been established as the new Imperial religion, a second ecumenical Council of Constantinople was convened in 381 CE in order to destroy all other usurping sects, including the Arian heresy. The Arians, like the Nazarenes, did not believe in the divinity of Jesus or the sanctity of the Virgin Birth and in order for the Church to remove the reality of a Jewish Messiah and his mother from the day-to-day work of the Empire, it was necessary that these became mystical figures rather than real ones, leaving the real power for the Emperor and his appointed bishops. It was therefore declared by the Church that the doctrine of the Trinity must be upheld by all believers. God was the Father, God was the Son and God was the Holy Ghost.

The first Ecumenical Council of Nicaea (now Iznik, Turkey), 325 CE. Depicting the condemnation of Arianism and the establishment of the Creed and the Festival of Easter.

28

The Nazarene and the Arian beliefs were naturally closer to the original Jewish ones whereby God was God and Jesus was a man, being the hereditary human Messiah of the Davidic succession, that is the King of the Jews through David, and his succession continued through his progeny. In 390 CE another creed emerged written in Greek which became known as the Apostles' Creed which reintroduced the concept of Jesus being the Son of God. Its timing was crucial because within a few short years Rome was to be ransacked by the Goths and the Western Empire fell into decline.

The Apostles' Creed

'I believe in God the Father Almighty, Maker of heaven and earth.

And in Jesus Christ his only Son our Lord; who was conceived by the Holy Ghost, born of the Virgin Mary, suffered under Pontius Pilate, was crucified, dead and buried; he descended into hell; the third day he rose again from the dead; he ascended into heaven, and sitteth on the right hand of God the Father Almighty; from thence he shall come to judge the quick and the dead.

I believe in the Holy Ghost; the holy Catholic Church; the communion of saints, the forgiveness of sins; the resurrection of the body; and the life everlasting.
Amen'
(Traditional English version)

'Credo in Deum Patrem omnipotentem; Creatorem coeli et terrae.
Et in Jesum Christum, Filium ejus unicum, Dominum nostrum; qui conceptus est de Spiritu Sancto, natus ex Maria virgine; Passus sub Pontio Pilato, crucifixus, mortuus, et sepultus, descendit ad inferna, tertia die resurrexit a mortuis; ascendit ad coelos; sedet ad dexteram Dei Patris omnipotentis; inde venturus (est) judicare vivos et mortuos. Credo in Spiritum Sanctum; sanctam ecclesiam catholicam; sanctorum communionem; remissionem peccatorum; carnis resurrectionem; vitam oeternam
Amen'
(Latin version circa 700 CE, still sung in monasteries today)

The Eastern Empire of Constantinople continued to flourish for another thousand years and evolved into the Russian and Greek Orthodox churches. Their liturgies, accordingly, were closer to the original Jewish forms of worship, which were choral.

THE MUSICAL FORMS OF EARLY CHRISTIAN WORSHIP

The formal language of the Roman Empire was almost universally Greek and as the Judaic-Christian missions began amongst the gentiles, they began incorporating Greek music forms, alongside the chanting of the Psalms from the Old Testament. Within a hundred years, as the church spread across the Roman Empire, most of its members were non-Jews who spoke Greek and lived in a Greek culture. This early church still retained some Jewish forms in its content, particularly that of chanting. After the legalisation of Christianity in the early fourth century CE, this music form and style developed into Byzantine music of the Greek Orthodox Church which was Christianity's first formal musical form. This Byzantine music was used throughout the Church through the seventh and eighth centuries. It was not, however, the only form to be used. In Egypt, in the Coptic Church and in the Celtic regions of Europe, there was a decidedly different form.

Mosaic, Byzantine, sixth century. Two female musicians. Mariamin (Syria).

The earliest Christian church had two Sabbath services: a synagogue-type service and a separate communion-type service and the two gradually became combined. Both the Divine Liturgy of the Orthodox Church and the Mass of the Roman Church had their origins in the liturgical form of Judaism. These specific forms, or liturgies of worship, were first seen in the Tabernacle of the early Israelites and were consummated in the temple worship which took place later in Jerusalem. In Judaism, there is a constant cycle of prayers, blessings and meals – daily, weekly, monthly and annually. The meals consist of breaking of bread and blessing of the cup and contain parallels with the Messianic feast. The synagogue worship in the time of Jesus had become a ritual family meal, with prayers said over it. The entire structure of the Last Supper, as recorded by St Luke, mirrors the meal liturgy as practised within Judaism of the time. For the average Israelite, the Temple was a place of worship only on certain days of the year, and during the Babylonian captivity, worshipping in the Temple was impossible and so a new form of worship came into being. This was patterned on temple worship but eliminated the sacrificial element. This form, known as synagogue worship, had a strong focus on teaching and remembrance. These two forms were included in the liturgy of the early Christian Church. The Apostles continued their Jewish worship on a daily basis and kept to the liturgical cycle of prayers at set hours of the day. The sacrificial side of this new form of Judaism supplanted the Temple sacrifices of animals to God through the Messiah himself being sacrificed in propitiation for all mankind's sins and thereafter for Christians there was no additional need for sacrifice.

The earliest and clearest reference to the liturgy of the early Christian church comes in Acts, the Book of the New Testament which chronicles the inception and growth of the early Church in Antioch, Greece. The Church in Antioch was the first gentile church outside Jerusalem and was established approximately 38 CE by Barnabas.

Illuminated manuscript showing the Apostle Barnabas.
From the 'Legende doree' by Jakobus de Voragine.

atouchierent point mais furent ense
ueliz des archens touz, entiers et il
couffrirt mort enuiron lan de noÿe
fte .ii.C.iiij.xx. et .vii.

de faint baruabe

Baruabe vault autrement dire ce
filz de celui qui viet ou filz de
coufolacio ou filz de propheite ou filz
conuenient il eft uns filz par .iii. foꝛ
pour .iiij. maneires de filianõ de li
il eft diet filz en efcripture par mã

Early Chants of the Christian Church

The liturgical rite of the Jerusalem church founded by James the Just, the brother of Jesus, became the foundation of the worship form and practice of all new churches. On this foundation was developed the form, practices, melodies and music that eventually became recognisable as the Gregorian chant.

The liturgical forms of early Christianity included many rites, all based on the liturgical practice of the 'mother church' in Jerusalem. Local variations developed over time through the development of prayers and other elements. Each local church developed its own unique musical form, built upon the ancient traditions. There are only fragmentary references to the liturgy in the early period in the Roman church. The common language of the Roman Empire was Greek and this was the language of the New Testament writings. Greek continued to be the language of the early Christian church until the time of Constantine and the change to Latin was only gradual after that time. The Latin language was used liturgically for the first time in the Roman 'province' of Africa. In this early period of Latin worship, there are written texts, notably the 'Gloria in Excelsis Deo' and the 'Te Deum', which were constructed as Psalms and called Psalmi Idiotici. The Gloria was first used in morning prayer before being added to the Mass.

Until the fall of Rome in 476 CE, public worship flourished with the celebration of divine worship copied from the style of the Imperial Court. The Council of Nicea held near Constantinople in 325 CE was the first ecumenical council which defined the doctrines of the early Roman Church. This was the Golden Age of the fathers of the Church whose writings were published, particularly those of St Ambrose, St Augustine and St Jerome. From these writings we can discover many details of the liturgy but still very little about the actual chant. In this early period the celebration of the Eucharistic Sacrifice of the Mass, which was a continuation of the early Judaic liturgy, began to change in order to commemorate the birth, death and resurrection of Jesus as the principle doctrinal mystery. Along with the daily celebration of the mystery of the Mass, the Sanctoral cycle included all feasts that had determinate dates and this included what was to become Christmas. Christmas itself was moved from one day to another until it was finally agreed that the festival of the birth of Sol Invictus, the Roman festival of the Unconquered Sun held around the end of December. December 25th would become Christmas and thus the official birthday of Jesus, who was now considered a divine being. During the services held on these feast days, prayers and chants were chosen from the Bible

appropriate to each feast day. The oldest collection of prayers that are still in existence are dated around 600 CE. These are the Leonine sacramentary.

Two streams of liturgical tradition began to evolve. The Alexandrian Roman tradition and the Gallican tradition. The term 'Gallican' is somewhat confusing in that it is used both generally to describe the liturgical family of Western rites outside the Alexandrian Roman tradition and specifically to indicate the liturgy of the region of Gaul. The Western tradition, most similar to the Alexandrian rite, is commonly called the Milanese or Ambrosian rite.

As the religion progressed its formalities, prayers and texts began to be sang as well as read. The early chanting was used at the great festivals of the Church such as Christmas and Easter. Unfortunately there is little information about the melodies that were sung in the early Church because

musical notation was not used. However, there were two methods of singing Psalms: responsorial and antiphonal. In responsorial singing the soloist sings a series of verses, each one followed by a response from the choir. In antiphonal singing the verses are sung alternately by soloist and then choir. From the fall of Rome to the rise of Charlemagne in 768 CE, Western Europe was in a state of turmoil. The civil order that Imperial Rome had brought was in a state of collapse and Teutonic tribes made regular incursions into various territories which resulted in the chaos of what is now called the Dark Ages. In many places the Bishop was the only recognised authority.

The Fathers of the Church Ambrose, Gregory and Augustine.

Left inner wing, inner side, of the Altar of St Jerome. On oakwood, 175 x 44.5cm.

THE RISE OF MONASTICISM

Monasticism was brought to the West from the Egyptian desert, particularly by St Anthony Eremite, St Martin of Tours and St Benedict. The rule of Benedict became the dominant form of monastic life in the West and specified the order of daily prayer that we now call the Divine Office.

St Benedict

Benedict was born the son of a Roman noble in Nursia, a small town near Spoleto in 480 CE. His early childhood was spent in Rome with his parents and he attended the schools with other members of the nobility. Instead of continuing with his higher studies, he left his father's house, wealth and books. He did not leave Rome at that time for the purpose of becoming a hermit but only to find a place away from the stressful and busy life of the eternal city. He took his old nurse with him and settled down to live in Enfide in the Simbrucini Mountains, about forty miles from Rome. It was here that he worked his first miracle and came to the attention of the local populace. Again, he fled, this time to the more rural district of Subiaco where he retired into a cave for three years.

On the death of the abbot of the local monastery the community came to him and begged him to take over the position. He agreed to become the new abbot but the experiment failed: the monks tried to poison him and he returned to his cave. From this time on his miracles became more and more frequent and many people attracted by his sanctity came to Subiaco to be under his spiritual guidance. In the valley he built twelve monasteries, in each of which he placed a superior with twelve monks. In the thirteenth one, Monte Cassino, he lived with twelve personally-chosen monks or disciples. He developed the Rule of Benedict which came to be used as the model rule for all monastic life. He died at Monte Cassino monastery in 543 CE.

St Benedict (480–546 CE) – the Founder of Western Monasticism. Illumnination, Italian, fifteenth-century. 'St. Benedict distributes the rules of his order'. From a choir book.

The monastic form of worship included singing around the clock. This was inspired by the continuous prayer of Egyptian hermits, marked by recitation of the Psalms from memory. St Benedict structured the Office to include the whole 150 Psalms of David sung during the course of the week. There were perpetual choirs throughout Europe that would be singing twenty-four hours a day, seven days a week in shifts. The Psalms themselves were complemented with antiphons, responsaries and hymns.

The different religious orders each had their own styles of chant. Benedictine chants were more elaborate than Dominican chants and generally sung at a higher pitch than Carthusian chant. The Benedictine order was perhaps the most well-known of all monastic orders in the world of Gregorian chant. St Benedict himself did not strictly speaking found an order. What he created was a rule of conduct by which to live by and many other monasteries other than Benedictine observed St Benedict's rule. The monastery of Subiaco was St Benedict's original foundation and he founded twelve other monasteries in the vicinity. He also founded the celebrated abbey of Monte Cassino which eventually became the centre from where his rule and institution spread. These fourteen monasteries are the only ones

that were founded during his lifetime. Unlike other orders the Benedictine order has no superiors or generals apart from the Pope himself. The order consists of what are practically a number of separate orders known as congregations. By the ninth century the Benedictines were the only form of monastic life throughout the whole of Western Europe, excepting in Scotland, Wales and Ireland where the Celtic monasteries retained their hold for another couple of centuries. Benedictine monasticism did not take hold of Eastern Europe in the same way. However, the Bohemiams and the Poles owed their conversion to Benedictine missionaries.

It was from the Benedictine monastery of St Andrew in Rome that St Augustine and his forty companions set forth in 595 CE on their mission to England, taking with them St Benedict's idea of the monastic life. These monasteries became the melting pot of chanting and it was through the combined work of the scribes and the singers that the Gregorian chant spread throughout Europe. Many of these hymns are attributed to St Ambrose and he is considered the person responsible for developing metrical and rhymed hymns.

St Ambrose

Ambrose was born Ambrosius in 340 CE at either Trier, Arles or Lyons. His father was Aurelius Ambrosius, a very high-ranking Roman official; he was Prefect of Gaul. Because of Ambrose's aristocratic background he was educated in Rome, particularly in the judicial system, and then entered the Imperial service in 365 CE. From there he became a governor and in 373 CE he was elected Bishop of Milan.

At the time he was alive hymns were unmetred and proselike. The Arians were using their own hymns to spread their ideology which refused to acknowledge the divinity of Jesus and which was therefore considered heretical by the Roman Empire. Ambrose countered this by setting his hymns to a metred form, which utilised the marching sound that the Roman soldiers used. Thus he was able to spread the Trinitarian theology and ensured the Emperor retained his divine status too.

When the Arians, protected by the Emperor's Arian mother Justina, wished to utilise the Basilica in Milan, Ambrose and his supporters occupied the building and steadfastly kept morale going using the power of hymns. The soldiers that had been sent to remove them subsequently failed. Throughout his life Ambrose

challenged the Emperors in order to discharge his duty to the church. Fortunately, he was so well-respected that they complied with his commands more often than not. In 387 CE Ambrose was to baptise Augustine who was to be canonised also. In April 397 CE Ambrose died but not before he left the world hymns such as 'Deus Creator Omnium' ('God That Created All') and 'Aeterne rerum conditor' ('Maker of All, Eternal King').

'They declare also that the people have been led astray by the strains of my hymns. I certainly do not deny it. That is a lofty strain, and there is nothing more powerful than it. For what has more power than the confession of the Trinity which is daily celebrated by the mouth of the whole people? All eagerly vie one with the other in confessing the faith, and know how to praise in verse the Father, Son, and Holy Spirit. So they all have become teachers, who scarcely could be disciples.'

(Sermon – St Ambrose)

St Ambrose by Tizian, real name Tiziano Vecelli,
c. 1477–1576. Oil on wood, Diameter 71 cm.
Former ceiling of church S. Spirito in Isola.

St Isadore

Isadore was born in Cartagena, Spain in approximately 560 CE. He received his education in the cathedral school of Seville. He succeeded his elder brother Leander as Bishop of Seville. At this time the ancient institutions and classical learning of the old Roman Empire were disappearing fast. A new civilisation was beginning in Spain, evolving from the blending of the tribal elements that made up its population. For two hundred years the Visigoths had ruled over Spain and unfortunately their barbarism threatened to put back the country's progress in terms of civilisation. St Isadore set himself the task of bringing together the various peoples who made up the Hispano-Gothic kingdom. The heresies of Arianism and Manichism were uprooted and eradicated. Like his brother Bishop Leander, he took a prominent role in the Councils of Toledo and Seville.

At the Council of Toledo in 633 CE he promoted the idea that all cathedral cities should have schools attached to them along the lines of the one already existing at Seville. This decree acted to counteract the growing influence of Gothic barbarism. His contribution to the educational movement of the time is profound and this policy of education was eventually made obligatory upon all the Bishops of Spain. He was the first Christian writer to essay the task of compiling for his co-religionists the sum total of human knowledge of the time. This encyclopaedia epitomised all knowledge both ancient and of the period, as well as recording liturgies, hymns and chants. It was St Isadore who brought the Mozarabic liturgy to Spain where it is still practised today. He died in 636 CE.

Right: A miracle-working banner of Baeza; St Isadore of Seville helps King Alphonso VII in the battle against the Moors in Almería. The banners were carried in all the battles during the Reconquista in Castile and León.

Illuminated manuscript, Spain, Mozarabic, 960 CE. The Temple of Solomon, from the Bible of 960.

39

THE LIFE OF A BENEDICTINE MONK

The goal of a Benedictine monk is to glorify God in all things. The Rule of Monasteries that St Benedict set down is strictly adhered to and the first duty is prayer. Also important is 'lectio divina' or holy reading and the monk must read the Scriptures and meditate on their wisdom on a daily basis. Within a Benedictine monastery one finds a great sense of community; having rejected all worldly goods and by recognising that having no possessions allows a freedom of the mind and soul, the monk looks only to God and the community for sustenance.

The Abbot acts as the disciplinary body within the monastery. The monk vows to stability, obedience and conversion to monastic life. It is not only obedience to the Abbot that is important but to all the other members within the community too. By laying down one's own will only then is it possible to do that of God. Celibacy is also a necessity, although this is not taken as a vow. When not in prayer, the monk must remain silent for only that way can he 'Listen' to the word of God. Black is the most frequent colour of the traditional monastic habit of a Benedictine order, although some variations are found, hence the term 'Black Friars'.

> '*As we progress in this way of life and in faith, we shall run on the path of God's commandments, our hearts overflowing with inexpressible delight of love.*'
>
> **(St Benedict)**

In the Monastery Courtyard. Tenth-century colour lithograph, undated illustration, from Ad. Lehmann's kulturgeschichtliche Bilder, Leipzig (F.E. Wachsmuth circa 1890).

41

The Eastern Rites

The liturgical practices of the Eastern Orthodox Church were founded on the practices of the Mother Church founded in St Jerusalem by James the Just, the brother of Jesus. This Judaic liturgical form was spread throughout the Mediterranean during the first years of Christianity by the Apostles. The common language and musical forms of the Roman Empire were Greek. While the liturgical languages of Italy eventually changed to Latin, of France to Gallic and that of the British Isles to Anglo-Saxon and then English, the Eastern nations retained the Greek form of liturgy, providing a living continuity and taking their rites back to the form of the early Christian church. The Eastern Orthodox church has experienced no reformation that changed the theological foundations of faith; neither has orthodoxy experienced a twentieth century reform both of the liturgical form and also its music as has the Roman Catholic Church. Therefore the Orthodox Church has a uniformity of the form that was in practice in the whole of the Christian church up to the sixth century CE. During the period of the fourth to sixth centuries, the shape of the Eastern Orthodox liturgy reached its final form under the guidance of St John Chrysostom. Generally speaking the worship of the Eastern Orthodox Church has always been in the vernacular, that is the local or indigenous language.

When St Cyril and St Methodius went as Greek missionaries to Russia in the tenth century they created a new alphabet, which is now called Cyrillic which translated both the Bible and the liturgy into the native language of Russia.

There are two main musical and liturgical traditions in the Eastern churches: Byzantine and Russian. Byzantine music has its pre-Christian origins in Greek music and like the Gallican chant is based on modes and chords described by Pythagoras. The earliest known hymn of this rite is called 'O Gladsome Night' which is sung every evening at vespers and has been dated pre-150 CE. The Byzantine church developed a very sophisticated form of chant and a very large body of liturgical material during the first millennia of its life. Its music is melodic and antiphonal, i.e. responsive. Byzantine music uses a unique analogue notation and has undergone several phases and refinements, the most recent being the simplification of the notation in 1881 CE.

The Russian musical tradition began when Greek music was brought to Russia by Christian missionaries in 998 CE. The earliest forms are called Znamenny and Kievan chant, both of which are Greek-sounding. The development of the former as an early unison Slavic

chant derives from the Slavic word 'znamia' meaning 'sign' and refers to the use of the musical notation in the chant. It reached its apex in the early seventeenth century. The trained singers of the city cathedral choir schools began embellishing the simple rural chants with more elaborate musical patterns. A single tone might even have as many as ninety or more short melodic patterns which could be selected by one singer as he improvised the music. These developed melodies reveal a deep expression of emotion contained therein as well as emphasising the vocal talents of the singer virtuoso. Russian liturgical music began its development as simple polyphony in the seventeenth century, under the influence of Polish music. It was further developed under Peter the Great who brought many musical styles from the West. Russian Orthodox music is usually more accessible to the Western ear because it utilises the same musical theory as Western music, whereas Byzantine uses Greek musical theory. Much of the Slavonic-speaking Orthodox Church, that is Serbian, Albanian and Armenian, follow the Russian musical tradition.

Although Bulgaria accepted Christianity 100 years or so before Russia, no musical manuscripts of that time have been located. Present-day Bulgarian singing is late Byzantine in style and quite unique although it has been adapted to the Slavonic language but with Bulgarian pronunciation. In the seventeenth century, hymns with the inscription 'Bulgarian chant' appeared in some Russian songbooks. Musicologists have noticed that the melodic chant of Bulgarian folksongs are closer to the spirit and character of Russian singing, even though the melodies are quite different from the Znamenny chant. The Bulgarian chants are more melismatic than recitative in style. Melodic lines are often repeated in succession through several textual lines of the song.

THE COPTIC ORTHODOX CHURCH

The Copts are the original Egyptians and the word 'Copt' itself is derived from the Greek word 'Aegyptus'. Descended from the Ancient Egyptian peoples, they are considered one of the most anthropologically pure races in the world. The Coptic Orthodox Church was founded by St Mark, a disciple of African origin and the writer of the earliest Gospel. He arrived in Alexandria sometime in the middle of the first century CE. St Mark won many converts, particularly because the Egyptian mind has always been religiously oriented. The Copts accepted Christianity very rapidly, to the extent that the Romans soon began to persecute them. Many of the early Coptic Christians were tortured and executed. The Alexandrian school was closed by the authorities and they suffered

severely as did all other Christians throughout the Roman Empire under the reign of Diocletian. So severe were these executions that the Copts take the beginning of their calendar from the day of Diocletian's military election as Emperor to mark the beginning of the era of the Coptic martyrs, known in the Western World as Anno Marterum (AM – or the Year of the Martyrs). The Coptic Church was forced to go underground and conducted its services in secret.

Throughout history the Coptic Church has played a significant role in defining and shaping Christian thought and doctrines. Alexandria was famous for having the largest library and museum in the world. It was established by Ptolemy Soter in 323 BCE and it was here that seventy legendary scholars from the Jewish community translated the Old Testament from Hebrew to Greek in 270 BCE. This monumental work is known today as the Septuagint. The monastic movement itself sprang into existence in Egypt and within a few decades had spread all over the Christian world. The characteristics of Coptic Monasticism are the urge to pray or chant

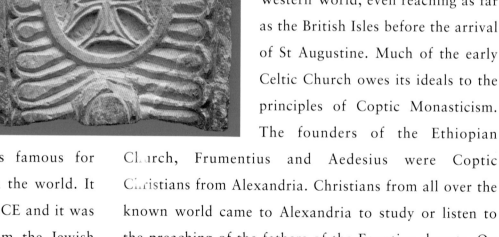

without ceasing, the desire to meditate on the Word of God and the subduing of worldly desires through poverty, fasting and celibacy. St Benedict took the precepts of Coptic monasticism and transformed it into the Rule of Benedict which became the benchmark of Christian mystical aspiration through monastic ideals.

Coptic missionaries helped to spread Christianity throughout the Western World, even reaching as far as the British Isles before the arrival of St Augustine. Much of the early Celtic Church owes its ideals to the principles of Coptic Monasticism. The founders of the Ethiopian Church, Frumentius and Aedesius were Coptic Christians from Alexandria. Christians from all over the known world came to Alexandria to study or listen to the preaching of the fathers of the Egyptian deserts. On returning to their own lands these students and pilgrims imported the spirituality, dogma and practice of the Orthodox Alexandrian Church.

An Egyptian copestone depicting a Coptic cross,
sixth or seventh-century, found at Luxor, 31 x 28 cm.

After the Council of Chalcedon the Copts were branded as Monophysites (see below) and a division in the Church occurred. The Orthodox Patriarch of Alexandria was deposed and exiled by the Western civil and ecclesiastical authorities. The Byzantine installed an Imperial Patriarch in Alexandria who was subject to the Emperor. This infuriated the Copts and they retaliated by electing a native rival Orthodox Patriarch. The Byzantine Christians persecuted the Monosyphite Copts and even massacred them within their churches. All attempts to reconcile the two divisions failed until the Islamic invasion of Egypt. By 642 CE Egypt had passed from the hands of the Roman Emperors of Constantinople to the Arab Moslems. The City of Alexandria had 4,000 palaces, 4,000 public baths, 400 theatres and over 40,000 inhabitants. When it was briefly recaptured by the Byzantines and then taken back by the Arabs the commander of the Islamic occupying forces ordered the city to be burnt to the ground. The great library and museum disappeared forever. The Copts have survived under Islamic rule and have been received in different ways in different times, from persecution to tolerance. Many Copts converted to Islam but today there are still about 6 million Copts and the liturgy is still celebrated in its original form.

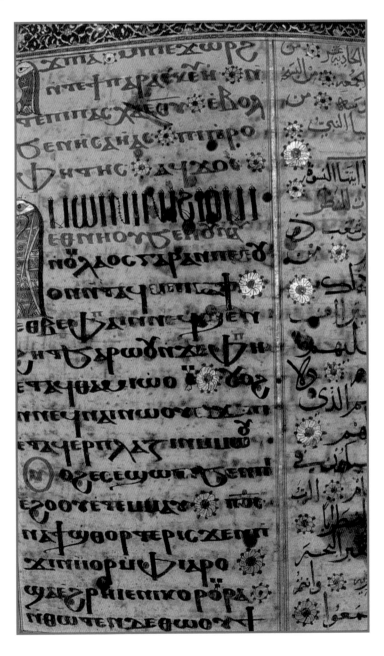

Illuminated page of text from a Coptic-Arab lesson, c. 1630.

Three liturgies are used within the Coptic Church. The liturgies of St Cyril and St Basil are from the Russian Orthodox Church, and the liturgy of St Gregory. According to tradition, the liturgy of St Cyril was originally that of St Mark that was transmitted orally until it reached St Cyril in the fifth century CE. It is regarded as the greatest, the oldest and the most complete liturgical text in existence and is unsurpassed as a work of religious literature. At present the Coptic Church is experiencing a revival in both its ministry in its homeland as well as those in other countries. Since the fall of colonialism in Africa, the African nations have been looking to the Coptic Church for religious leadership and spiritual guidance, since it is the only indigenous African church. At last the Coptic Church is no longer isolated and recently has been meeting with the Roman Catholic and other Christian denominations.

In the Coptic Church it is vocal music rather than instrumental music which is used. The hymns which are sung in the Coptic Church are the hymns of the Ancient Egyptians. Even though the Copts embraced Christianity, the belief did not affect or change their musical heritage which dated back to the rule of the Pharaohs. New words coloured the music but the melodies and rhythms were retained. Archaeologists have been able to match up the position of the face muscles on early temple paintings in Egypt with those of modern Coptic cantors when they are performing their liturgy and this has proven that little has changed. The hand signs used by the conductors in these ancient frescoes are still used to teach vocal Church music today.

One papyrus called the 'Bahnasa hymn', dating from the third century CE, is considered to be the oldest transcribed Coptic hymn.

> *'All God's creatures should not stand in silence,*
> *nor the lightning stars can hide, all the wave-filling*
> *rivers, praise the Father, the Son and the Holy Ghost*
> *and all hosts participate with them Amen Amen'*
> **(The Bahnasa Hymn)**

46

ETHIOPIAN CHRISTIANITY

Ethiopia was referred to by the ancient Egyptians as 'Ta-Neter', 'the Land of God'. Legend has it that Christianity came to Ethiopia in the early fourth century CE when a Christian philosopher named Meropius was shipwrecked on his way to India. Meropius died but his two wards Frumentius and Aedesius were taken to meet King Ella Amida and became his servants. They were permitted to proselytise their religion and when Frumentius returned to Alexandria, the Bishop of Alexandria agreed to send missionaries back with him and he ordained Frumentius as the first Bishop of the Ethiopian Orthodox Church. His mission was successful and with the support of the King Ezana Ethiopia became a Christian nation.

At the end of the fifth century, nine monks arrived from Alexandria and introduced monasticism into Ethiopia which has remained a dominant feature of the Ethiopian Church to this day. They brought with them the Doctrine that makes the Ethiopian and Coptic Church different from other branches of Christianity. This Doctrine, called Monophysite, believes that the Divine and Human Natures of Jesus were fused into a single nature at his birth. The Ecumenical Council of Chalcedon in 451 CE, on the other hand, distinguished between the Divine Nature of Christ and his Human Nature, declaring that Jesus had two distinct natures and so declared the Monophysite Doctrine of Ethiopia heretical. Since that time along with the Ethiopian and Coptic Church the smaller churches in Syria, Turkey and Armenia have remained Monophysite in their beliefs. The nine monks who were also Monophysites, translated the Bible into Ge'ez, the language of the Ethiopian peoples of the time and although this language is no longer a written one or used for everyday speech, it is still used in the liturgy of the Church.

During the seventh century Islamic conquests cut the Ethiopians off from the rest of the world, except for the Ethiopian monastery in Jerusalem. The Prophet Mohammed had instructed his followers to be kind to the Ethiopians since they had sheltered a number of his companions. Although the country was one of the first to officially embrace Islam, relationships deteriorated between the Moslems and the Ethiopian Christians and the country fell into a Dark Age. In the twelfth century it re-emerged under the leadership of a new dynasty, although they were accused of being usurpers. However, the King, Lalibela, built ten churches in his capital which were carved out of the rockside. These churches are now considered one of the wonders of the world.

In the sixteenth century Ethiopia was again overrun by the armies of Islam but the following century the King Suseynos became a Roman Catholic in the hope of forging advantageous military alliances with Europe. He prohibited the Ethiopian Islamic custom of circumcision and made the Sabbath a holy day again. Ethiopian Orthodox Christianity lost considerable ground in the nineteenth century, again due to the expansion of Islam. The church suffered from a lack of leadership and the populace found the Orthodox fasts difficult to maintain and had no understanding of the Ge'ez language of the liturgy. The fortunes of the Church reversed in the latter half of the nineteenth century when once again Ethiopia was centralised by a succession of kings who were genuinely devout and looked after the interests of the Church.

A Coptic parchment from Ethiopia with

a depiction of an angel and magical text.

In the twentieth century Ethiopia saw the influx of Roman Catholic and Protestant missionaries and is now a land of churches. Most of its churches are octagonal in shape; the roundness is reflected through the Ethiopian Church liturgy with its emphasis of the holy mysteries in the centre of the church and with the participation of multiple priests and lay clergy, chanting and drumming in a circle. Like the churches of the Knights Templar the churches of the Ethiopian Church consist of three concentric rings. The central one is the sanctuary and contains the Ark, representing the Ark of the Covenant (which is claimed to reside to this day in Ethiopia). This is where the priests and the Emperor conduct the Eucharist from. The middle ring contains the congregation and the outermost ring is called the choir and is where the priests chant the Scriptures using Ge'ez and play musical instruments that accompany the hymns. The Ethiopian Church has retained many of the Jewish practices. Circumcision is a normal procedure and devout Ethiopian Christians keep the Sabbath on Saturday as well on Sunday. An Ark is an essential part of the Church service and it is carried out for festivals. A sacrifice of a lamb or a goat is also performed in times of great need such as sickness.

St Yared

St Yared was born in April 505 CE in the city of Axum in Ethiopia. He struggled with his academic studies until he made a plea to God. He was enlightened by watching a small insect struggle to climb over a tree trunk. On its seventh attempt it finally succeeded and this encouraged St Yared to continue with his studies and to also succeed. Later he received a vision of three birds: a red one, a yellow one and a green one. These represented the Trinity of God but also they stood for the three melodies that he would incorporate into the liturgy of the Ethiopian Church. Until that time singing loudly was forbidden. Yared went back to Axum and entered the Church of Zion there where the Sacred Ark of the Covenant lay. He sang praise to God in Ge'ez and used Aryam, a song rhythm. Whilst he was caught up in his visions he heard the angels playing musical instruments – a large flute, a cistrum, a large drum, a one-stringed violin and a harp. He had these instruments made and used them to accompany his hymns. With the blessing of the Chief Priest of the Church he set to work and composed a large number of chants for the liturgy. He also invented a notational system. Yared composed hymns for each of the four seasons, for festivals, Sabbaths, the days of the

angels, prophets, martyrs and for the righteous. He divided his chants into four parts, each with its own melody. He also wrote a book called the 'Degua' which in Ge'ez means 'Songs of Higher Knowledge'. The book is also called 'Mahleti Yared' which means the 'Treasure of Yared'.

The three modes of chanting used in the Ethiopian church are known respectively as Ge'ez (green) which is the plainchant for ordinary days, Izil (yellow) is a more measured beat for funerals and Ararai (red) which is a lighter form for the great festivals. The Ethiopian flag still retains these colours to this day. His musical innovations were centuries old before Europeans created the present musical notation with its seven letters of the alphabet. After creating his chants in the three modes he also created ten notes: Yizet, Deret, Reqreq, Difat, Chiret, Quinet, Hidet, Qurt, Dirs and Anbir. These ten are referred to as the Seraye. Yared's notation comprised of dashes, curves and dots.

Although he passed away in 571 CE there is a legend that he did not really die and that he continues to this day to preach and teach anonymously in Ethiopia.

THE WESTERN RITES

Old Roman

During the fourth century CE the communion Antiphon, originally taken from Psalm 33, was sung during communion. The Antiphon 'taste and see the goodness of the Lord' alternated with the verses of the Psalm. Later that century Psalmody was sung after the Epistle. The next change came in the entrance rite which consisted of the Introit, Kyrie and Gloria in Excelsis Deo which became added to the Mass before the readings. This Introit also consisted of an Antiphon that alternated with the verse of a Psalm. Also the Offertory was sung during the preparation of the bread and wine at the altar. Later the Alleluia which was originally sung before the Gospel at Easter, became used throughout the rest of the year, except during Lent. At some point during the seventh century the Roman singers of the Papal Masses began composing distinct chants for each part of the Mass throughout the year. This project was completed by the beginning of the eighth century.

Ambrosian

Ambrosian, also known as Milanese chant, is the oldest of the Western forms of chanting. It is attributed to the work of St Ambrose, Bishop of Milan (374–97 CE). Despite these early origins, the Milanese chant is usually identified with the Lombard Kingdom. Charlemagne became King of Lombardy by conquest in 774 CE and his dynasty ruled Italy until 962 CE. The Carolingian insistence on Gregorian chant was ineffective in Lombardy and again at the Council of Trento in the sixteenth century when the many local variants on Gregorian chant were standardised, Milan was able to retain its unique rite because of its antiquity. The sung Proper parts of the Milanese mass are Ingressa (Introit), Psalmellus (Gradual), Alleluia, a chant following the Gospel, Offertorium (Offertory), Confractorium (replacing Agnus Dei) and Transitorium.

The capital of the Duchy of Lombardy was Benevento and this was established at the same time as the Lombard kingdom in the north of Italy. Both were formed when the Lombards drove the Ostrogoths out of Italy. The Lombards in both these areas regarded their liturgies as having descended from the early Milanese rite and is therefore a variation on it. One of the most important liturgical centres was the monastery of Monte Casino, St Benedict's first monastery and the centre of Benedictine monasticism.

Mozarabic chants

This term refers to the old Spanish rite, sometimes called the Visigothic rite which remained in use in Spain during the time of the Moorish rule. The Arian Visigoths, who were driven from France into Spain, became Catholic in 587 CE. When the Moslems overran Spain a remnant of this Visigothic kingdom was left along the northern coast of Spain and the zenith of this old Spanish rite was reached in the seventh century. The Verona Orationale is a collection of office prayers that was taken to Italy for safekeeping during the Islamic invasion of Spain. This document dating from around 700 CE, as well as showing the literary style of the old Spanish rite also contains marginal cues of chant texts.

In this document there are notations as to the music used in the chants but they are indecipherable. When Moorish Spain was reconquered, French monks and bishops immediately moved there and the old Spanish rite was abolished in favour of the Roman rite with its Gregorian chant. The old Spanish rite became known as the Mozarabic rite because it had continued to be used during the time of Arab rule.

*Gozzoli, Benozzo 1420–1497. 'Scenes from the life
of St Augustine', 1564/65. Fresco. San Gimignano,
Church S. Agostino, choir.*

Celtic and English chants

The Celtic rite, of which no documentation remains in existence, is thought of to be similar to the Gallican rite. When St Augustine arrived in Britain in 597 CE to convert the Anglo-Saxons, he brought with him the Roman rite. By 664 CE, the Celtic Christians and the Roman Christians became reconciled at the Synod of Whitby. Celtic rites continued in Scotland and Ireland until the twelfth century.

When St Augustine converted the Angles and Saxons to Roman Catholicism they followed the Roman rite. The term Sarum chant used in the Church of England today does not refer to a distinct rite. The Sarum chant includes chants particular to numerous local saints. By the thirteenth century the use of Sarum (the Salisbury diocese) was used all over England. In the nineteenth century the Anglo-Catholic movement in the Church of England published chants of the Sarum use as their liturgical heritage. These had previously been published in 1528 and 1532 during the reign of Henry VIII.

Gallican

The Gallican rite and its chants originated in Gaul in the fifth century CE. It had its heyday after the Merovingian king Clovis, who was an Arian Christian, became baptised into the Roman Church in 496 CE. The Merovingian kings of France had their origins amongst the Benjaminites who moved from the Holy Land firstly to Greece and then up the river Rhône. Their own pagan rites were connected with the Nazarene rite and they grew their hair long as did other Nazarenes such as Sampson and Jesus himself and they particularly venerated Mary. Before converting to Arian Christianity, a form which did not hold Jesus to be divine, they worshipped Artemis, the Arcadian Mother Goddess, whose totem was the bear. The Merovingians intermarried with the Visigoths and from their seat in France were able to rule much of Europe. Their reign came to an end during the time of Charlemagne who suppressed the Gallican rite because all other rites outside of the Roman rite were seen as heretical. This also meant that they refused to acknowledge the Holy Roman Emperor as divine. The event that led to the repertory of the Gregorian chant was the visit of Pope Stephen II to Paris in 754 CE. He was there to ask for King Pepin's aid against the Lombards in Italy. King Pepin had usurped the Merovingian Frankish throne in 751 CE, having asked the previous Pope to decide whether a king should be one who occupies a throne or one who exercises power. The Merovingian kings had been effete and weak and were unable to rule. Pepin took control. He was anointed King of the Franks during Pope Stephen's visit. This was the first time that a king had been anointed by a religious leader. Until that point the king ruled by divine right.

King Pepin ordered the Roman chant to be sung in his Frankish kingdom and it took repeated injunctions from him and his successor Charlemagne to accomplish this radical change. Cantors were brought from Rome to teach the chants to the Franks. By about 800 CE Frankish scribes had copied complete manuals of the texts of the Mass from the Roman sources, of which two survive to this day. Unfortunately, they do not contain musical notation.

Pepin the Younger and Pope Stephen II defeat Aistulf.
Copper engraving by Matthäus Merian (1593–1650).
From Johann Ludwig Gottfried, Historische Chronica,
Frankfurt (M. Merian) 1630.

The Franks made two major contributions to Gregorian chanting: they fitted the chants into the ancient Greek system of eight modes which were being used in Byzantine chant. In the Byzantine system these modes are called 'Echoi' and are melodic types. The division of Gregorian chant into eight modes was adapted from this. These eight modes functioned as scales to which individual chants were assigned. Each mode is characterised by a tonic note and a dominant note which made their tonality distinctive. These eight modes had already been used throughout Europe in secular music, each mode being able to evoke a particular emotion. This division of Western chant into eight modes, also known as Church Modes, was only adopted by the Frankish Gregorian chant and this is one of the properties that makes the Gregorian chant repertory unique and different from all the other forms of chant. The modes are as follows:

Table showing the division of Western chant into eight modes

MODES	RANGE OF NOTES		GALLICAN NAME	GREEK NAME
I.	DEFG abcd	Authentic	Protus authentus	Phrygian
II.	ABCDEFGa	Plagal	Protus plagis	Hypodorian
III.	EFGabcde	Authentic	Deuterus authentus	Dorian
IV.	BCDEFGab	Authentic	Deuterus plagis	Mixolydian
V.	FGabcdef	Plagal	Tritus authentus	Hypolydian
VI.	CDEFGabc	Authentic	Tritus plagis	Lydian
VII.	Gabcdefg	Plagal	Tetrardus authentus	Hypophrygian
VIII.	DEFGabcd	Plagal	Tetrardus plagis	Hypomixolydian

The final note is the one on which the melody finishes. If the melody was consistently above the final note (finalis), then it is considered authentic. However, if the melody is mainly below the final note, then it is considered plagal. The modes were believed to alter people's state of morality: to play outside the Church modes was deemed as a way to immorality.

In the late ninth century treatise 'Alia Musica', the modal terminology was incorrectly reapplied to the Gregorian repertory as follows:

The Incorrect Modes

MODE NO	GREEK NAME
I	Dorian
II	Hypodorian
III	Phrygian
IV	Hypophrygian
V	Lydian
VI	Hypolydian
VII	Mixolydian
VIII	Hypomixolydian

However, the Gregorian repertory was conceived before the adoption of this eight-mode Greek system. There is also evidence of some alteration of Gregorian melodies to make them conform to this eight-mode system. Some early sources do contain antiphons for Psalms which certainly do not conform to the system. One way of telling if this is so is to do with the final note as early music only allowed four notes to end with, these being D, E, F and G.

Further mode names were added in the fifteenth century by Glareanus and these were also based on Ancient Greek place names. These were called Aeolian, Locrian and Ionian, all played on the white notes of the modern-day keyboard. They begin on A, B and C respectively. Glareanus posited that the Locrian mode to explain chants that fell outside of the eight Church mode system which ended on B. This Locrian mode would have been a problem in the Middle Ages in that it would imply the existence of a mode with a final on B and a recitation note on F with these two notes being a diminished fifth apart. This pitch difference was considered diabolical. Interestingly, the Locrian mode occurs in much of modern rock music, also considered at various times to be the Devil's music.

There are early Gregorian sources that also contain antiphons for Psalms outside of the modal system which are probably descended from responsorial Psalm forms in the early church. The Old Roman chant appears to have a greater fluidity than the later Frankish chant which adopted the rigid eight-mode system. The Old Roman chant was much more of an oral tradition and so constantly evolving as it passed from choir to choir, person-to-person, whereas the Frankish system was written down and therefore frozen in its development.

Charlemagne

Charles the Great, King of the Franks and First Sovereign of the Christian Empire of the West was born on 2nd April 742 CE. At the time of his birth his father Pepin the Short was Mayor of the Palace of Childeric the Third, the last Merovingian King of the Franks. In 752 CE, Pepin appealed to Pope Zachary to recognise that, as Mayor of the Palace, he was the one who actually ruled the Frankish Empire rather than Childeric who spent his time engaged in frivolous pursuits. Pope Zachary agreed with him and two years later the next Pope, Stephen III, journeyed across the Alps for the purpose of anointing with the purpose of kingship not only Pepin but his sons Charles and Carloman. The Pope then exerted a binding promise from the Christian Frankish hierarchy under the gravest spiritual penalties never to choose their kings from any other family. At that time primogeniture did not hold in the Frankish laws of succession; their monarchy was elected although eligibility was limited to any male member of one privileged family. This was known as the Merovingian dynasty or Sorcerer Kings. Suddenly, on 28th July 754 CE the House of Arnulph (Charlemagne's bloodline) was, by a solemn act of the Supreme Pontiff, established upon the throne that until then had been occupied by the House of Merovae. From that point on the monarchs were anointed by the Pope rather than be kings by divine blood. It is interesting to note that the dynasty of the Kings of Israel also ran through a divine bloodline and it has been suggested in modern times that the Merovingians themselves were members of a divine bloodline that went back through Jesus, Moses and then to the divine pharaohs of Egypt. The tradition of chanting, of course, follows the same route.

'Crowning of Charlemagne' by Christian Meichelt
after Johann Friedrich Dieterich (1787–1846).
Aquatint etching, coloured later.

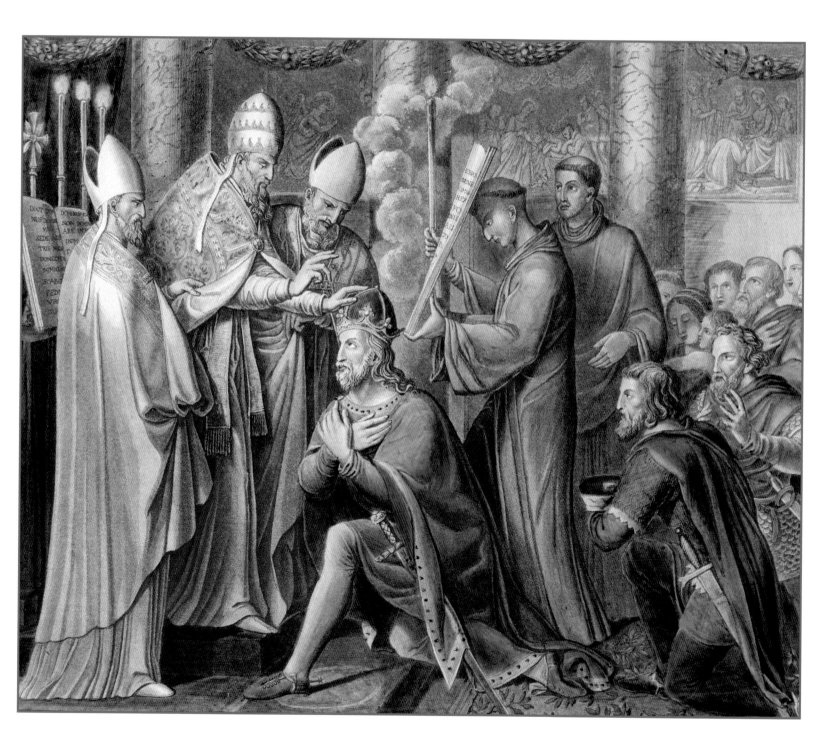

When Pepin died the two brothers divided the kingdom between themselves. The share which Charles inherited consisted of all of Austrasia, most of Neustria and all of Aquitaine except the south-east corner. In 771 CE his brother Carloman II died and left all of his lands and wealth to Charles who became the sole King of the Franks. The name Charlemagne is from the Old French. Two years later Pope Hadrian II appealed for his aid against another Teutonic tribe called the Lombards who were running rampant in northern Italy and had begun to invade the Papal States. Charlemagne besieged and took Pavia, the powerbase of the Lombards, and then took the crown of Lombardy. When he returned to his capital at Aachen he began a series of fifty-three campaigns, all led in person, designed to expand his Empire by conquering and Christianising Bavaria and Saxony. He also defended Italy from the Saracens and the borders of what is now France from the ever-invading Moors from Spain. The Saxons on his Eastern front were not just pagan; they fought with untiring ferocity. They hated Christianity and any other form of authority. Charlemagne waged eighteen campaigns against them before they capitulated. He gave them a choice between Baptism into the Roman Church or death and then beheaded 4,500 Saxon rebels in one day.

His reputation as the greatest warrior king of the Dark Ages was well-founded and although he had little formal education himself he could speak Old Teutonic as well as literary Latin and understood Greek. His court was the home to a number of leading scholars, composers and musicians. At his court the font Carolingian minuscule was developed which became the basis for modern printing.

On Christmas Day in the year 800 CE Pope Leo III crowned Charlemagne as Emperor of the West in St Peter's Basilica, Rome, in gratitude for the King having rescued him and saving Rome and the Papacy from the heathens. Charlemagne henceforth attempted to revive the glories of the old Roman Empire by founding what later came to be called the Holy Roman Empire which covered the greater part of Europe. Until his death in 814 CE, he continued to be a great patron of the arts and scholarship. He founded an academy at Aachen, his capital city, where he was also buried and was canonised at the request of Frederick Barbarosa in 1165 CE.

'My heart is steadfast, O God;
I will sing and make music with all my soul.
Awake, harp and lyre!
I will awaken the dawn.
I will praise you, O Lord, among the nations;
I will sing of you among the peoples.
For great is your love, higher than the heavens;
your faithfulness reaches to the skies.
Be exalted, O God, above the heavens,
and let your glory be over all the earth.'

(Psalm 108)

Charlemagne supervises the building of Aachen Minster.
fifteenth-century illumination, from: Les grandes chroniques
des rois de France.

'The Triumph of Charlemagne', fresco from the series of Ariost frescos. Rome Cassino Massimo, Ariost-Hall. Schnorr von Carolsfeld, Julius 1794–1874.

61

The Age of the

Gregorian Chant (800–1500 CE)

'PANGE, LINGUA gloriosi

Corporis mysterium,

Sanguinisque pretiosi,

quem in mundi pretium

fructus ventris generosi

Rex effudit Gentium.'

'Sing, my tongue, the Saviour's glory,

of His flesh the mystery sing;

of the Blood, all price exceeding,

shed by our immortal King,

destined, for the world's redemption,

from a noble womb to spring.'

(St Thomas Aquinas)

THE GREGORIAN CHANT

regorian chant is purely functional music designed to enhance the service of worship and in itself is objective and impersonal. Its objective is to focus the listener and participant on the act of worship. Although traditionally the chant is in Latin, it is now used in many other languages.

The Gregorian chant consists of a single, unaccompanied melodic line constructed according to tonal patterns, different from those forming the major and minor scales. The most basic and earliest form of Gregorian chant, as with all church modes, is diatonic in nature. The diatonic scale is found on the white notes of the modern-day keyboard and stems from the Greek musical modes; it is

comprised of three sets of major triads. A major triad is formed from three notes which have the frequency ratios 4:5:6 when sounded together.

For example using the octave of C it is possible to create three major triads:

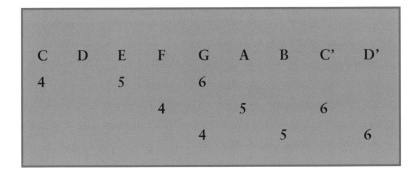

C	D	E	F	G	A	B	C'	D'
4		5		6				
			4		5		6	
				4		5		6

The root note or tonic is the note which gives the name of the tone or major chord.

Gregorian chant was originally intended to be sung by men in worship but from the fourth century CE the women of the convents also began to use it. The chant itself is monophonic and modal. It is usually sung in a flexible rhythm, based on the text, without regular accentuation or beat. This is because, as written, no fixed temporal values are given for the notes. There is also no manuscript or treatise in existence which lays down specific instructions for its exact performance. The Benedictine monks of Solesmes in France state that the natural rhythm of Latin prose is the 'vital determinant of chant rhythm'.

NEUME NOTATION

The history of Gregorian chant is the early history of Western music theory. What distinguishes Gregorian chant from all the chants that preceded it was that from 900 CE onwards it was written down. It was the invention of music notation that for the first time in history allowed the melodies themselves to be written down. Chant is notated using neumes which are written above and alongside the text. This early form of musical notation, from which our modern systems are derived, was used to indicate the shape of the breath and therefore melody, 'neume' coming from the Greek word gesture or breath of air.

It was during the reigns of Pepin and Charlemagne that the Franks began to learn the Roman chant. At the beginning of the ninth century CE, Frankish scholars had copied many of the sung texts from the Mass but had not yet managed to notate them according to melody. The Franks then began to fit the Roman chants into the Greek eight-mode system which was also being used in Byzantine chant. To start with, early neume notation was

limited in the information it conveyed as it only showed up (acutus) and down (gravis) within a text and a certain amount of the rhythm, as can be seen from surviving manuscripts from the mid-ninth century. The early neumes which only conveyed the rhythm of the chant had been replaced with those that mainly dealt with the rise and fall of the melody. This largely meant that the tune had to be passed on from person to person and memory rather than only through literary means. No staff was used, thus making early chant decipherment a very difficult practice.

By the early part of the tenth century, neumes are to be found through complete Graduals and it is only from the tenth century that we have complete copies of the Gregorian chant repertories in which the texts are fully neumated. Different systems were used by different monasteries which meant that the information could not be shared

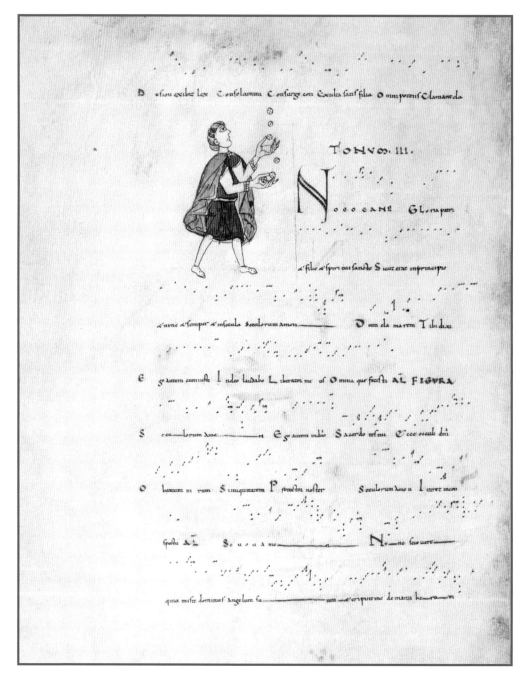

between different orders. Gradually, neume notation evolved and became more complex in order to convey the information necessary to accurately record and so preserve a chant on paper. Neumes were added that showed gradation of rise or fall, or a combination so that the metrical nature of a chant and all its melody could be read off the page. The eleventh century saw a universal system for neume notation in place and at last a four-line staff was introduced. Whereas the early neumes preserved the rhythms but not the melody, when new notational methods were created then the original melodies had already been lost and so sadly only the later centuries of chant melody were preserved.

Neumes are between one to four notes, all of which fall upon the same syllable of the text. Each interval pattern has its own name and there are twenty-two names, all in Latin for each of these.

Punctum

A single note.

Virga

A single note.

Podatus

One note is written above another note, with the bottom note being sung first.

Clivis

One note is written above another, similar to Podatus, except the higher note is sung first.

Scandicus

Three or more notes going upwards.

Salicus

Three or more notes going upwards but with the middle note being slightly lengthened.

Neumes (musical notes) with text and an illustration
(a man juggling with pebbles). From a liturgical manuscript
(John of Abbatis Villa).

Climacus

Three or more notes going downwards.

Torculus (pes flexus)

Three notes that start going up and then go down again.

Porrectus (flexus resupinus)

A high note, followed by a low note and then a high note again.

Scandicus flexus

Four notes that start going upwards and then go downwards again.

Porrectus flexus

A high note followed by a low note twice.

Climacus resupinus

Four notes that start by going downwards and then go upwards again.

Torculus resupinus

Four notes that go downwards, upwards, downwards again and then upwards.

Pes subbipunctus

Four notes with the second note going up, the third going down to the original and then the final note down again.

Virga subtripunctus

Four notes in a row going downwards.

Virga praetripunctus

Four notes in a row going upwards.

The Liquescent Neumes

These neumes demand much more vocal control and precision in their achievement within chant.

Epiphonus (liquescent podatus)

Cephalicus (liquescent flexa)

Pinnosa (liquescent torculus)

Porrectus liquescens

Scandicus liquescens

Quilisma

The term Gregorian chant is used as an umbrella term for plainchant and credited to Pope Gregory I. Gregory has been credited with many things, including the writing and organising of the repertory of plainchants in use at the time. He is also credited with founding the first choir school in Rome and organising the annual cycle of liturgical readings but mostly he is credited with establishing the Roman church's authority over the secular rulers of Rome. Many of the aspects of worship attributed to him in later centuries were an attempt to build up and support the primacy of the Papacy. The chant that was actually used in Gregory's time is now known as Old Roman and was an oral tradition so sadly little of it has survived to the present day. The 'Gregorian' chants that we know of today are in fact Frankish. Two centuries after Gregory, Charlemagne had asked Rome to send them singing teachers but the Frankish choirs made many alterations and adapted the chants to their own peculiar ways of singing. The Gregorian chant that was written down by the Franks would have been dissimilar to that heard in Rome and modern Gregorian chant could be better be described as Carolingian rather than Gregorian.

Pope Gregory I

Pope Gregory was born in 540 CE and before he became a Benedictine monk, he had been a government official. He was elected Pope in September 590 CE, after the death of Pelagius II who was himself a great reforming Pope. Like

Pelagius, Gregory continued to resist the power of the Lombards who were threatening to overrun Italy. His success put much of Italy under direct Papal rule and these lands became known as the Patrimony of St Peter. The revenue and power that these lands provided now gave the Pope one of the most powerful positions in Italy as well as Europe.

A twelfth-century colour illustration depicting Pope Gregory I dictating his homilies to his secretary while under the influence and inspiration of the Holy Spirit, who, in the shape of a dove, sits on his shoulder.

Gregory was a supreme administrator and also an advocate for the Doctrine of Celibacy for priests. He expanded the power of the religious orders and gave them independence from local church officials, making them answerable only to the Pope on a personal basis. Gregory was also one of the first Popes to believe that religious relics were effective in healing or conferring spiritual powers and their popularity can be traced back to him. His changes in the Roman liturgy are perhaps what he is most renowned for and he is believed to be responsible for arranging the Gregorian chants which became the central pieces of music in religious services.

As Supreme Patriarch of the West, Gregory's jurisdiction embraced the three Prefectures of Italy, the two Gauls and Eastern Illyricum. His Papal reign lasted 13 years and 6 months until his death in March 604 CE.

St Gregory at his writing desk.

Ivory panel, Reichenau, end of tenth century.

Height 20.5 cm.

Chant Modifications

Tropes

Troping is the term used when a chant is expanded through either adding words to an existing chant melisma (a passage of several notes that is sung to one syllable of text) or adding music and so extending an existing chant. The Tropes are able to stand alone as they are coherent pieces both musically and textually, but they are designed to enhance an existing chant. It was during the tenth through to the twelfth centuries that troping flourished but at the Council of Trento these were deleted from the liturgy although musical tropes still continued to be used, for example in the Kyries. The most famous of the 'Tropers' was named Notker Balbulus (840–912 CE).

Antiphons

An Antiphon is a chant sung in alteration with verses of a Psalm and its concluding doxology. Originally this alternate singing took place between two choirs. For this reason, early Antiphons are simple, syllabic or neumatic settings in a rather limited range with a simple rhythm. When soloists assumed responsibility for much of the liturgical singing it was then that Antiphons took on a more ornate and florid form. Antiphons are the most frequently encountered type of chant with over 1,200 listed as part of the current Antihphonale.

Sequences

The Sequence is sung in the Mass, immediately following the Alleluia. Thousands of sequences were composed during the Middle Ages and this chant varied from region to region according to local customs. However, after the Council of Trento, only four sequences were approved, namely 'Dies irae' ('Day of Wrath') which is sung in the Requiem Mass, 'Victimae paschali laudes' ('Praises to the paschal victim') which is sung at Easter, 'Lauda Sion' ('Zion, praise') which is sung at Corpus Christi and 'Veni Sanctus Spiritus' ('Come Holy Spirit') which is sung on Whit Sunday.

Early Sequences were extensive melismas, normally prose, that were substituted for the Jubilus at the repetition of the Alleluia section after the verse. However, they soon became independent chants that were not linked to an Alleluia and started to take on a poetic form. By the twelfth century onwards they had matured to a form which consisted of isosyllabic couplets, that is, the same number of syllables in a couplet, and each line sung to the same melody but each couplet varied from the next one in both length and melody.

Conducti

Conducti were songs in Latin marked chiefly by their liberation from any standard characteristic. They could by rhymed, rhythmic or metrical and some resembled hymns, some sequences, some had refrains and others use different music for each and every line. The only regularities were that the lines tended to be of similar length. The music was more melismatic than syllabic. Conducti were used during liturgical processions or wherever the priest or other parties were 'conducted' from place to place.

Sequences and tropes may have started life as a singer's memory aid. In the introduction to a collection of his sequences, Notker Balbalus (the Stammerer, 840–912 CE), a monk of the St Gall monastery in Switzerland, tells the story of a French monk who sought refuge at St Gall in 862, following the Norman sacking of his monastery at Jumieges, in Normandy. Notker noticed that the monk's antiphonary (chant book) showed new words fitted to melodies that St Gall sang on a single syllable. Struck by the notion that words might help him to memorise the long wordless melodies, Notker revised the St Gall chants accordingly. The melody lines with new words were called tropes.

Notker Balbulus

Notker Balbulus was born in about 840 CE in Jonswill in Switzerland. He joined the monastic school of St Gall, Switzerland and became a monk (Notker was given as a title to St Gall monks), having been educated by Tuitilo. Balbulus held a number of positions within the monastery. His main role was as a teacher but he was also a well-respected and prolific poet and author and held the position of librarian for some time. He introduced the Sequence, a new species of religious lyric, into the Teutonic nations. Prior to this it had been the custom to prolong the Alleluia in the Mass before the Gospel, by modulating through a carefully harmonised series of tones. Balbulus learned how to fit the separate syllables of a Latin text to the tones of this jubilation. Between 881 and 887 CE Notker dedicated a collection of sequences to Bishop Liutward of Vercelli. He was nicknamed 'The Stammerer' because he was petitely built and had a stutter to his voice. Balbulus died in 912 CE and was beatified in 1512.

First page of the Easter sequence 'Laudes Salvatori' by Notker Balbulus from collection: 'Liber hymnorum' (860–887) with neumes. Manuscript, Einsiedeln monastery. (Photo after facsimile).

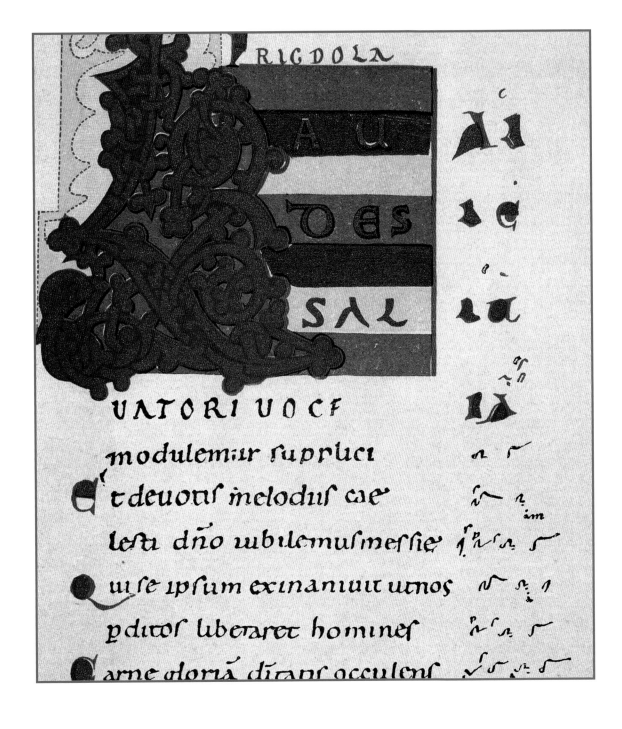

ORGANUM AND THE BEGINNINGS OF POLYPHONY

Polyphony is the term given to that type of music that results from the simultaneous combination of two or more independent melodic lines. The polyphony used in liturgical music from the late ninth to the early fourteenth century CE was called 'organum', meaning organised or planned music. The earliest known treatises that have survived are called 'musica enchiriadis' (music manual) and 'scolica enchiriadis' (commentary manual). 'Scolica' was a Latin term denoting the marginal comments that scholars wrote in text books. The organum consisted of a chant melody named 'vox principalis' (principal voice) with one, two or three additional voice parts derived by duplicating the chant melody in parallel motion at a specified harmonic interval that was considered as a consonance. This duplicate voice was called 'vox organalis' (planned voice). The creation of this planned voice was permitted at three levels of consonance of which there were three types. The first is simple organum and this was produced by singing an exact duplicate of the chant melody in strict parallel motion, at the interval of an octave, a fifth, or a fourth below the original chant. The second composite organum was produced by either doubling at the octave with both or one of the voice parts of a simple organum. The third type has two subdivisions: parallel organum and modified parallel organum. The former is strictly homophonic with parallel fourths, fifths and eighths and has only one note per syllable. The latter is modified so that each phrase begins in unison although it spreads to parallel fourths with the principal voice lying above the planned voice but the phrase then contracts again to finish on the unison. They converge again at the end of the phrase, which is known as 'occursus' (meeting).

STAFF NOTATION

Music is a form of human communication as ancient as language itself. Very early in history the need for a reliable system of musical notation was felt. Up until quite recently most music belonged to an oral tradition, that is, it was passed from one performer to another by memory and repetition. Until visual notation came about, pieces of music changed as they were passed on, in the same way as the children's game of Whispers will alter a whole sentence's meaning. During the course of centuries and cultures pieces of music became unrecognisable from their origins. Alongside written language, systems of musical notation were developed in order to pass along a more consistent information than the oral tradition allowed for. Very little is known about the music of the ancient world and their notation systems

are virtually unknown to us. Because the ancient peoples of Sumeria and Egypt devised writing in order to make written communication more consistent across their empires, they devised symbols to accompany the system of hand signals that they used to indicate the pitch, tone and shape of the melody. In the early third century BCE the Chinese invented a sophisticated system of notation. These early systems were made up of symbols to represent separate vocal syllables, a form of sol-misation (soh-fah-la) and also instructions for playing specific instruments – an early form of tablature.

In the West, the use of letters of the alphabet to represent notes of the scale dates back to Ancient Greece and was well established by 500 BCE. Letter names were given to whole tones of the diatonic scale (the white notes) and inflections of a semi-tone or even a quarter tone could be expressed by movement of the letter symbols.

Two different systems of letters were used to write down the instrumental and vocal music. Bothius applied the first fifteen letters of the Greek alphabet to notes. This system was also capable of indicating the rhythmic value of a piece of music. However, until the ninth century, we have no other written music available in history documents or in archaeological evidence available for us to study. At this time Christianity was the driving force behind all social and artistic advances in the Western world.

In the sixth and seventh century the monastic communities of Ireland contributed greatly to art and design with manuscripts like the 'Book of Kells' and were responsible for the founding of the monastery of St Gall. A large number of manuscripts of notated music was also produced there.

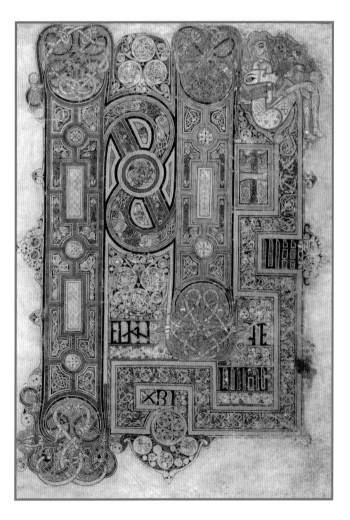

Book of Kells, page bearing ornate initial of the St Mark's Gospel.

The Ancient Greeks notated pictures by letter names. This continued to be used until the eleventh century CE. As discussed previously, the earliest notated Western manuscripts date from the ninth century and were produced at the monastery of St Gall. The chant music was written in 'accent neumes'. The choir master's hand movements as he conducted were used to indicate melodic movement. In the ninth century, Aquitaine notation began to be used. This is called 'point neumes'. Dots were placed above the words of the text and by the eleventh century some scribes drew a line across the page and used coloured inks and letters to designate pitches. Commonly, a red line was used for F and a yellow line was used for C. These lines are the forerunner of the modern staff. Notation differed from monastery to monastery and scribe to scribe. The best known are Sangallian, from the monastery of St Gall, Aquitanian, French, Norman, Beneventan, Paleo-Frankish, Messine and Gothic. These types of notation lasted until the fourteenth century but by the

High Middle Ages, the experiments of dissatisfied music theorists had produced a more precise form of notation. The first person of note to recognise the value of using a staff notation to designate definite pitches was Guido D'Arezzo.

Guido D'Arezzo

Guido D'Arezzo was born in 990 CE and entered the Benedictine abbey at Pomposa, Italy, as a monk. He soon acquired a reputation for teaching choristers to learn new chants quickly. He was invited to Rome in 1028 CE to explain his methods and systems of notation to Pope John XIX. D'Arezzo advocated learning chants by reading music rather than by rote. His method of teaching required the choristers to memorise a chant, each of the first six phases of the chant beginning with a different pitch and a different syllable of text. Successively the six initial pitches form the C hexachord. The singers were expected to relate these six syllable pitch combinations to the notes of any chant.

The hexachord consists of six notes and corresponds to the first six notes of the modern-day major scale. There are three types of hexachord: hexachord durum, hexachord naturale and hexachord molle. The six syllables that D'Arezzo used were taken from the first lines of the Hymn to St John the Baptist and are Ut, Re, Mi, Fa, Sol and La. The pitch syllable combinations D'Arezzo used for sight singing have since become standard but have been expanded to include a seventh pitch, Si.

D'Arezzo stressed the importance of ear training and of letting the ear be the final judge when selecting melodic intervals. When a singer encountered a melody whose range exceeded six notes the requisite additional range was acquired through mutation which is the process of moving from one hexachord to another. This is comparable with the modern process of modulating from one key to another via a pivot chord.

Guido d'Arezzo, the Italian Benedictine and music theorist who founded the system of musical notation. Chalk lithograph, nineteenth-century, by O. Puccioni.

By the middle of the fifteenth century a system similar to present-day rhythmic notation had evolved. Certain patternings of neumes were used to represent the various rhythmic modes. Franco of Cologne created a clear indication for each note of its exact rhythmic length and selected certain neumes to represent tones of long and short duration. The long value was equal to three of each of the shorter ones and were called 'ligatures' because the individual notes appeared to have been tied together. Mensural notation, in which each note has a specific time value, became a necessity for the development of polyphony. Philippe De Vitry (1291–1361 CE) in his music theory text 'Ars Nova' expanded Franco's system and qualified duple divisions of the long and short notes. This was shown visually by different combinations of a dot inside a circle or half circle and the symbols for perfect time (nine/four time) and imperfect time (6/4 time) used the alchemical symbols for gold and silver who were believed to be perfection and near-perfection of metals. During this time 9/4 and 6/4 timings were considered the most preferable in all music. The modern symbol for 4//4 or common time, also derived from this form of notation which was a half circle with no dot in the centre.

Numbers with the appearance of fractions were also used to indicate that one proportion of rhythmic value was

being substituted for another. Modern time signatures, placed at the beginning of the staff, evolved from this. It was not until the seventeenth century that bar lines, expression signs and Italian terms such as 'pizzicato' were used to indicate the tempo and dynamics. With the adoption of equal temperament and major and minor keys, signatures showing a major key or its relevant minor became standard.

By about 1700 CE our modern system of notation using a stave of five lines, as opposed to the four used in Plainchant, became firmly established. A stave of five lines for vocal music was taken up in France and a stave of six lines was utilised in Italy. The modern version of music notation became firmly established across Western cultural boundaries due to the widespread use of printing.

The musical notation of Henry Purcell (1659–1695), in his own handwriting. Showing the modern system of notation using a stave of five lines for vocal mucic.

THE SCHOOLS

St Martial of Limoges

The Abbey of St Martial de Limoges was founded in 848 CE at the site of the tomb of St Martial, the first Bishop of Limoges in Aquitaine. From 930–1130 CE, a school of poets and composers flourished there and the twelfth century saw the rise of Aquitanian polyphony. The Abbey became a library of liturgical manuscripts from the south of France. The surviving manuscripts are the most comprehensive collection of Western Frankish tropes, sequences and songs. The notation used in them ranges from early point and accent neumes to the basic square notation used in the twelfth century. Four of these manuscripts contain a total of sixty-nine pieces of twelfth century polyphony. The music arising out of St Martial Abbey was of two styles: 'melismatic organum' and 'descant organum'.

At this time the 'tenere' (tenor) was often the main voice in a chant and sang the long notes. The organal voice sang above these notes, and used a flowing melody of shorter notes. The organal voice, and therefore second voice, would add ornamental flourishes to a single syllable and so this was known as melismatic organum or florid voice. Therefore, the chant had a more melodic sound. The descant organum is simply the older style whereby the voices are set note for note to each other and the chant is more rhythmic.

The Versus is a setting of a sacred poem of rhymed Latin verse and was extemporised each time. This kind of song was used as a liturgical addition on important feast days, particularly those relating to the incarnation and the Virgin birth. The musical setting of Versus is descant. The Versus is one of the earliest polyphonic musical forms not based on chant. The oldest surviving manuscript of this Aquitanian polyphony has survived from the beginning of the twelfth century.

Santiago de Compostella

Santiago de Compostella is located in north-west Spain and was perhaps the most important pilgrimage shrine during the Middle Ages. Pilgrimages made to it were comparable with those made to Canterbury and Rome. Choirs of pilgrims from all over Europe kept up a perpetual chant at the cathedral altar. They also brought with them and performed on all kinds of instruments. The 'Liber Sancti Jacobi' (The Book of St James) contains monophonic and polyphonic music and demonstrates that all sections of the Ordinary,

except the Credo, were troped, that is extended. The polyphonic settings of these sacred rhymed Latin poems used for processionals were labelled 'conductus'.

The Cathedral of Santiago de Compostella. View of the west facade – so-called Obradoiro (built 1738–50 by Fernando Cazas y Nóva).

The Paris School of Notre Dame

When Rome conquered Gaul in 53 BCE, they established a settlement on an island in the River Seine and named it Lutetia. The temple on the island was dedicated to Jupiter and by the fourth century CE the Merovingian monarchs had renamed it Paris in commemoration of one of their Greek forebears. By the twelfth century Paris was the cultural and intellectual leader of Europe. The original island that the Romans had colonised was now called Île de la Cité and was the heart of the city of Paris. The temple of Jupiter had been replaced first by a Christian basilica and a Romanesque church called the Cathedral of Notre Dame, which had been constructed in Carolingian times. The right bank of the Seine had become a trade centre but the left bank was dominated by a university and became a centre for learning. During this time Latin was the official language of the church, schools, universities and bureaucratic processes. Kings and high-ranking church officials worked together to increase the prestige and wealth of both the church and the state. All learning was under the jurisdiction of the Papacy.

The twelfth and thirteenth centuries were the time of the great cathedral constructions of France. These buildings were considered to be the physical representation of the heavenly kingdom on Earth. The light admitted into the sanctuary through the stained glass windows was seen to be divine. Religion and the supernatural dominated medieval life and so the music that was used in the cathedral was intended to heighten this aura of otherworldliness within the parameter of the cathedral. The Gregorian chant was the supreme embodiment of this.

In 1160 CE the Bishop of Paris, Maurice de Sully, decided to replace the Carolingian building of Notre Dame with a great cathedral. This was to be called the Cathedral of Notre Dame and designed and built in the new gothic style. The construction process began in 1190 CE and took until 1250 CE to complete. During the building of the cathedral all buildings in the periphery were demolished. The new cathedral was distinctive in many aspects: the vault was over 108 feet high and Notre Dame was the first structure to use the flying buttress which is a support built against and projecting from a wall to resist the pressure from within. Large stained glass windows were utilised to increase the amount of light entering and to transform it. The particular glass holds a mystery to modern glass manufacturers to this day as it is very translucent. The Rose Window, which is 32 feet in diameter, appears as a gigantic halo for the sculpture of the Virgin and Child and its base. The acoustic properties added a whole new dimension to the already mystical Gregorian chant.

When the Cathedral of Notre Dame was being constructed, there were a group of composers active in Paris, producing polyphonic liturgical music. Léonine and Pérotin were considered master composers of organum. The latter was considered the best composer of descant. He also composed three and four voice organum and monophonic and polyphonic conducti. One of the most significant contributions that the Parisian school of composers made to chant music was the use of rhythmic modes and modal notation in their creation of polyphonic settings of chant. In the thirteenth century composers had found a way of notating rhythms, something that was badly needed. There were six rhythmic modes which were identified by numbers. In the last quarter of the twelfth century Aquitanian neumes were given more definite shapes and were written in square forms. These rhythmic modes were discussed in many treatises of the thirteenth century and gradually the six forms were settled upon.

Notre Dame Cathedral in Paris.

ACOUSTICS OF CATHEDRALS

It is important to remember that the Gregorian chant can best be appreciated and understood in the context that it was originally designed for. The Roman chant that developed into Gregorian chant was essentially the Latin liturgy of Rome, grafted onto a Frankish tradition of song that in turn took its melodies from the Merovingian era. The Merovingians traced their roots back to the Tribe of Benjamin in Israel and were known to worship the mother goddess Astarte, Queen of Heaven. When the great Gothic cathedrals of France were begun during the Carolingian era, each was named Notre Dame (Our Lady) and the chanting in them would have been predominantly Marian chanting, i.e. chants in adoration of Mary Queen of Heaven.

When we think of Gothic architecture images of grandiose structures come to mind. These cathedrals were not austere places but were adorned with gargoyles, stained glass windows, gold leaf images, filigree stone and the whole structure was a triumph of light and space over gravity. The architecture of these cathedrals came at a time when the Knights Templar had returned from the Holy Land bearing with them architectural drawings that they had found underneath the Temple of Jerusalem. These architectural miracles had in turn been inherited from the Master Builders of Egypt. The secrets and the building techniques had been lost; the Knights Templar brought a renaissance of architecture with them. Within these great buildings there were perpetual choirs chanting their praises to God and the Virgin, all night and day.

These undertakings in France could easily be likened to the modern-day space programme in terms of huge numbers of people with diverse disciplines: engineering, mathematics, sacred geometry and acoustics came together to create these amazing places. Projects like these are rare in history. Today people are in great awe of the Great Pyramid of Cheops in Egypt, Stonehenge and the Mayan temples but when these more recent temples of excellence were in their full glory with the incense burning, the candles flickering, the choirs of angels singing inside a space so unlike any other that the people would experience in their lives, the effect must have been miraculous to say the least. In their desire to reflect the glories of God, each cathedral reached higher into the sky and included more light, colour and gold in their adornment. This complete mystical experience that is so unknown in the modern world could be achieved by any ordinary person on a daily basis. The cathedral never slept. The same would be true of the great temples of the Egyptians.

Notre Dame (begun in 1163).

Rose window of the southern

transept (c. 1270).

The chanting that began to be called Gregorian matched the visual spectacle with an audio one. The acoustics of the cathedral were tuned particularly to the male voice and the sound reverberated around the structure. If you did not know that there was a choir of men and boys singing, you could easily believe that you had entered Heaven and were listening to a choir of angels. This was the pinnacle of the Roman Catholic culture but there were many who felt that these expensive and time-consuming projects merely appealed to the vanity of man, rather than God, and distracted from the real Christian work of feeding the poor and healing the sick. At that time in France, the Cistercian monks led by Bernard of Claireveaux, whose mystical vision led him to believe that the visual opulence of architecture was a distraction from divine truth, developed an aesthetic architecture of his abbeys and monasteries which expressed these beliefs visually. They were often stark and unadorned. Although the architecture of sacred geometry simply conveyed its perfection, again the interior acoustics were tuned so that the sound of the choir would be suspended in space all around the listener. The sound of a pin dropping could be heard. Bernard's convictions were strong enough to threaten a schism between Rome and France but ironically Bernard was canonised for his great missionary work and appears in Dante's 'Paradiso' where St Bernard reveals the full splendour of the glory of God to Dante.

As the austerities of Protestantism took over European society, so the cathedrals were gradually silenced. It has taken until recent times to gain any technical understanding of Gregorian chant at all. We may know how it was written but where it is sung affects it tremendously. Gregorian chant is sung in unison which means that all the voices in the choir are singing the same notes at the same time. It is the imperfectness of the human ability to sustain the right note at the right time that gives it its full sound. If men and women, or men and boys, are singing together they are not singing in the same pitch, as women and boys usually sing higher than the men, even an octave or more. Three important factors are prevalent within the Gregorian chant: intonation, resonance and pitch relationships. Intonation is what differs praying from speaking. Sometimes this is called incantation and is a single pitch sustained throughout the prayer, Psalm or song. Many Anglican rituals are performed by reciting in a single pitch. Sometimes the pitch is dropped at the end of each sentence.

As previously mentioned, the context of the sound produced by chant in the kind of building reinforces its

resonance. Nowadays, electronics can be utilised to create an echo chamber or reverberation. The spaces that Gregorian chant were sung in were all built as natural echo chambers and reverberant acoustic spaces. Usually any intoned pitch produces overtones and although these are not noticed consciously, in a cathedral these overtones are greatly magnified and can produce remarkable effects, effects that would be perceived as mystical. In performance this effect is called doubling and it happens in Gregorian chant whenever men and women or men and children sing together. This is sometimes referred to as singing in parallel because the women will be singing the same melody as the men but at a higher octave, yet the two parts blend so well that it still sounds as if it is of one voice, i.e. unison singing.

When reciting, some pitches have the power to penetrate into the listener's mind more intensely than a choir. The sound of both the choir and the congregation singing together in unison is like no other musical experience and again, it has often been described as transcendant or mystical. Each cathedral or abbey was tuned to a different key and so when the choir sings in that key, even more amplification and reverberation are present. When the choir sings in another key, a sense of dissonance and displacement can occur.

It is also known to choristers that after singing several Psalms in the same pitch, that melody reverberates in the memory for an hour or more. The whole body is affected by the frequencies of the tones. The Psalms of David lend themselves perfectly to the recitation rhythms, i.e. monotonal in their original Hebrew. When translated into Latin, there were more syllables present in each sentence and the melody was woven around them in order to accommodate this.

In a Gregorian melody, almost all the pitches are repeated and many musical loops are formed. The pitches change persistently and their patterns do the same and it is rare to find a regular pattern in a chant. This avoidance of pattern within Gregorian chant seems to generate a sense of otherworldiness about it. However, there is an exception to this rule where exact and obvious repetition of the melody is found in the format of melisma.

Chants were differentiated not only by form (sequence, trope, conductus, hymn) and the number of notes per syllable, but also by style. Hildegard of Bingen's smooth flow of notes, with relatively few pauses or jumps to notes much higher or lower, contrasts with the Gregorian style of chant, which is marked by comparatively short, repeated melodic phrases and by frequent fourths.

Hildegard of Bingen

Hildegard was born in 1098 CE in Böckelheim on the River Nahe in what is now Germany and was the daughter of a knight. Like many daughters of the lesser nobility, when she was eight years old she was sent to Mount Disibode to be educated. The monastery, in the Celtic tradition, housed both men and women. She was placed under the care of Jutta, a nun. Hildegard was afflicted with ill health throughout her childhood and at various times lost both her ability to walk and her sight. Although she learnt to read and sing the Latin Psalms she never learned to write.

Hildegard received prophetic visions, which she was able to contemplate particularly when she was on her sickbed. Jutta pointed this out to a neighbouring monk but this information was initially ignored. When Hildegard turned eighteen she became a nun in the Order of St Benedict and when her mentor Sister Jutta died in 1136 CE, Hildegard was appointed Superior of the convent. Aspirants began to flock to the convent but Hildegard was to receive a divine command which ordered her to found a new religious community in Rupertsburg, near Bingen. Hildegard oversaw its construction.

An illuminated page from Scivias (Know the ways of the Lord).The Christian virtues before the wall of the Law of the Old Testament.

It was not until the age of forty that Hildegard again received a divine command to set down her visions. She first wrote three books, with a monk acting as her scribe, which contained twenty-six visions in all. She continued to set down her work and wrote a further six books as well as seventy poems, seventy-two hymns and their melodies and a play set to music called 'Ordo Virtutum'. The 'Ordo Virtutum' was written in dramatic verse and has eighty-two melodies within what are the neumatic settings of the text.

Two of her books featured medical and anatomical information and she also wrote a treatise on herbs. In terms of her music books, the notation had only just been developed to a point where her music was able to be written down in a way that we can understand today. In the 1150s she assembled some of her works under the title 'Symphonie armonie celestium revelationum' which means 'Harmonic Symphonies of Celestial Revelation'. The music is in early German neumes written on four-line staves with F and or C letter-clef identification. The music of Hildegard relies on melodic patterns which are part of her compositional repertoire. The compositions move from syllabic to highly melismatic ones. Thankfully, much of her music has been recently recorded for all

to enjoy. Today she is considered to be a musical genius ahead of her time.

She died in 1179 CE and although she was not officially canonised she is considered to be a saint and has a feast day in her honour on 17th September.

Inspiration of Hildegard, woodcut, 1524 from 'The legend of the blessed virgin Saint Hildegard', 1524 with later colouring.

Studium Divinitatis

'Studium divinitatis
in laudibus excelsis osculum pacis
Ursule virgini cum turba sua
in omnibus populis dedit.
Unde quocumque venientes perrexerunt,
velut cum gudio celestis paradisi
suscepte sunt,
quia in religione morum honorifice
apparuerunt.

De patria etiam earum et de aliis regionibus
viri religiosi et sapientes ipsis adiuncti sunt,
que eas in virginea custodia servabant,
et qui eis in omnibus ministrabant.

Deus enim in prima muliere presignavit,
ut mulier a viri custodia nutriretur.
Aer enim volat
et cum omnibus creaturis officia sua exercet,
et firmamentum eum sustinet,
ac aer in viribus istius pascitur.
Et ideo puelle iste

per summum virum sustentabantur,
vexillate in regali prole virginee nature
Deus enim rorem in illas misit,
de quo multiplex fama crevit,
ita quod omnes populi exhac honorabili fama
velut cibum gustabant.
Se diabolus in invidia
sua instud irrisit,
qua nullum opus Dei
intactum dimisit.'

Divine Devotion

'Divine devotion
bestowed the kiss of Peace
upon the Virgin Ursula,
with her flock,
and before all people.
And thus,
wherever they went they were welcomed,
for the joy of the celestial paradise,
which they received,
was the honor of their religious life,
made manifest.

From their homeland and from other lands

religious men and sages joined them,

keeping them in holy care,

and ministering to them in all ways.

Therefore God in the first woman foretold

that woman by man is protected and so nourished.

Even as the air flies,

attending to all creatures,

so too does the firmament of heaven sustain it,

and the air is nourished through this enfoldment

And for that reason these young girls

were sustained by the supreme man

for their holy nature is the standard of royal descent.

For truly God showered them in a dew,

from which grew many aspects of fame,

thus all people partook of this honorable fame

as nourishment.

But the devil in his envy

mocked that of the Divine,

thus none of God's works

remained unspoilt.'

(Hildegard of Bingen)

An illuminated page from Scivias (Know the ways of the Lord).
A priest celebrates communion; the Christians in the light
and in the darkness. The original twelfth-century manuscript
was formerly in Wiesbaden but disappeared during the
Second World War.

Other famous composers were: Adam of St Victor (d. 1192 CE), writing from the Abbey of St Victor just outside Paris; Hermannus Contractus (the Cripple, 1031–54 CE), from the monastery at Reichenau, who produced a 'Salve Regina' as well as the 'Alma Redemptoris Mater' (popular enough in the Middle Ages to rate a mention in Chaucer's 'The Prioress's Tale'); Abelard (1079–1142 CE), who composed a book of hymns for the use of Heloise's nuns and his own monks. St Thomas Aquinas wrote not only 'Lauda Sion' (adapting music from a popular song by Adam de la Halle) but also the hymn 'Anima Christi', still familiar to Catholics.

Thomas Aquinas

Thomas Aquinas was born into a noble family in the middle of the 1220s CE. His father was Landulph, Count of Aquino and his mother was Theodora, Countess of Teano. The family were related to the Emperor's Henry IV and Frederick II as well as to the Kings of Aragon, Castille and France. At the age of five, as was the custom amongst the nobility, Thomas was sent to receive his first training from the Benedictine monks of Monte Cassino. He was diligent in study and devoted to prayers and meditation. His talents were such that in 1236 CE he went to the University of Naples. He studied grammar, logic and the natural sciences. The educational custom of the time divided the liberal arts into two courses: the 'Trivium' which covered grammar, logic and rhetoric and the 'Quadrivium' which comprised mathematics, geometry, astronomy and music.

In the early 1240s Thomas received the habit of the Order of St Dominic in Naples and his peers were surprised that a young man of such noble birth should don the garb of a poor mendicant. His mother was particularly fretful and went immediately to Naples to talk him out of it. However, the Dominicans sent him to Rome and then on to Paris. At the insistence of Theodora, her other sons were sent to capture the errant Thomas and confined him in the fortress of St Giovanni for two years. The whole family, using various means, destroyed his vocation. Thomas, however, managed to utilise his time spent in captivity to his advantage: he procured some books and set about studying them. After two years, he escaped and immediately rejoined the Dominicans. He pronounced his vows and was sent to Rome. Pope Innocent IV blessed him and the Fourth Master General of the Teutonic Order took him to Paris where he was placed under the tutelage of Albertus Magnus, the most renowned professor of their Order.

In 1252 CE the Order appointed Thomas Sub-Regent of the Dominican Stadium in Paris. This is where he began his public career. His teaching soon attracted the attention of both the professors and students alike. From this time onwards, the life of Thomas was dedicated to praying, preaching, writing, pilgrimage and most of all teaching. His life was also that of an ecstatic and he was often caught up in Divine visionary trances. In December 1273 CE he laid his pen aside and said 'I can do no more. Such secrets have been revealed to me that all I have written until now appears to be of little value'. Gregory X called a General Council to be held in Leon on 1st May 1274 CE and invited Thomas Aquinas to participate. Thomas set out on foot in January of 1274 but collapsed and was taken to the house of his niece, Countess Francesca Ceccano. The Cistercian monastery of Fossa Nuova pressed him to accept their hospitality and he was taken by carriage to stay there. On entering the monastery he said 'This is my rest for ever and ever: here will I dwell, for I have chosen it.' (Psalm 131: 14). His words foretold his death and he passed away on 7th March 1274 CE. He was canonised by John XXII on 18th July 1323 CE.

'Soul of Christ, be my sanctification.
Body of Christ, be my salvation.
Blood of Christ, fill all my veins.
Water of Christ's side, fill all my veins.
Passion of Christ, my comfort be;
O good Jesus, listen to me,
In Thy wounds I dare to hide
Never to be parted from Thy side;
Guard me should the foe assail me,
Call me when my life shall fail me,
Bid me come to Thee above
With Thy saints to sing Thy love –
World without end.
Amen.'

Anima Christi (Body of Christ)
(Traditional Prayer of St Thomas Aquinas)

Saint Thomas Aquinas as Doctor of the Church.

Panel painting, 1363, by Francesco Traini.

Tempera on wood. Pisa, Church of S.Caterina.

The Roman Catholic Liturgy

Meetings of the early Christian church commonly featured either a re-enactment of the Lord's Supper or Psalm-singing, Scripture-reading and prayer. These religious observances developed into the two principal services of the Roman Catholic Church, respectively the Mass and the Offices. By the ninth century the liturgy for these services was fully developed. In 1014 CE, the Vatican's formal acceptance of the Credo into the ordinary of the Mass occurred. The recommendations of the Council of Trento in 1545–63 CE caused deletion of many sequences from the Mass. At the Second Vatican Council in 1962–5 CE, permission was given for the use of the vernacular rather than the Latin language and this instigated the reform of the liturgy and its music. The use of Latin in the service has now almost become obsolete.

The calendar for the liturgical year traditionally comprised two concurrent cycles, known as the Proper of the Time and the Proper of the Saints. The Proper of the Time consists of the liturgical observance of all Sundays of the year and the commemoration of the principal events in the life of Jesus. Some of these events are fixed dates such as Christmas, whereas others are moveable such as Easter. The Proper of the Saints concerns the honouring of certain Saints on certain specified dates in accordance the Church's system of feasts. The liturgical year is as follows:

Advent	A penitential season beginning the fourth Sunday before Christmas
Christmas	Twelve Days from Christmas Eve to Epiphany (6th January)
After Epiphany	From 7th January until 9 weeks before Easter
Pre-Lent	Beginning nine weeks before Easter until Ash Wednesday
Lent	A penitential season from Ash Wednesday to Easter
Easter tide	From Easter to Pentecost including Ascension Thursday (based on the first Sunday following the full moon after the Spring Equinox)
Pentecost	Seven weeks after Easter (Whit Sunday)
Trinity	From the first Sunday after Pentecost to the fourth Sunday before Christmas

Christmas mass at St Peter's Basilica, 1950, Rome, Italy.

The Offices

The Canonical Hours, also called the Offices, constitute the prescribed daily round of worship and prayer in all monastic communities, whether recited privately or sung in public. The fixed order for the offices was set by the rule of St Benedict in the sixth century and is as follows:

Matins	During the night but after midnight
Lauds	Before dawn
Prime	6 o'clock in the morning
Terce	9 o'clock in the morning
Sext	Noon
None	3 o'clock in the afternoon
Vespers	Sunset
Complin	Before retiring for the night

These Offices were intended to mark three hours intervals commencing with Matins just after midnight and concluding with Complin at 9 o'clock in the evening.

The most important musical Offices are Vespers, Matins, Lauds and Complin, in that order. All canonical Hours contain Scripture readings with responses, hymn singing and Psalms verses with their antiphons. An antiphon is a chant sung in alteration with verses of a Psalm and its concluding doxology (a short verse praising God). Some offices contain canticles which like Psalms are sung in alteration with antiphons. Old Testament canticles are sung in Matins and Lauds, whereas New Testament canticles are sung in Lauds and compline. Polyphony was sung in Vespers from medieval times and was admitted in Matins and Lauds during the last three days of Holy Week.

There are four 'Marian antiphons' (Marian referring to Mary), each assigned to each of the principal divisions of the year. The first is Alma Redemptoris Mater (Gracious Mother of the Redeemer) which is used from the Saturday before Advent to and including 1st February. The second is Ave Regina Caelorum (Hail, Queen of Heaven) from 2nd February to the Wednesday of Holy Week. Regina Caeli laetare (Rejoice, Queen of Heaven) which is from Easter Sunday to and including the Friday after Pentecost. The fourth is Salve Regina (Hail Queen) which runs from Trinity to the Saturday before Advent.

THE MASS

In both the Judaic liturgy and the early Christian liturgy the sharing of bread and wine were essential components. Prayers and the singing of Psalms also figured prominently at these gatherings. As these early Judaic Christian communities increased in size, special religious services were held on Sabbath morning, later in

recognition as the first day of the week as the Lord's day, the service was held on a Sunday morning.

By the second century this rite had become known as the Eucharist, from the Greek 'Eucharista' meaning 'I give thanks'. Scripture passages and the singing of Psalms became an integral part of the Christian ritual and non-Christians were encouraged to attend services, in contrast to the Jewish rite to which only Jews were permitted to attend. This was the major Nazarene heresy. For the first time, non-Jews were allowed to be involved with Jewish ritual. During the first four centuries of the Christian church, the services started with a greeting and continued with three Scripture readings; one from the Old Testament, one from the Epistles and one from the Gospels. The service was interspersed with Psalms, a short address by the priest leading the service, followed by a prayer. The second half of the service, called the Eucharist or Holy Communion, began with the offering of gifts of bread and wine for consecration. The prayers that were offered developed into the preface and canon and included the Sanctus, taken from Isaiah 6:3. The Benedictus (blessing) which is part of the chant was added at a later date. The congregation would then partake of the bread and wine and following another prayer the congregation was dismissed.

By 375 CE the service was being called 'Missa'. This was derived from the Latin 'Ite, Missa est' which are the words used to conclude the service 'Go for the message has been sent forth' with the response from the congregation 'Deo gratis' or 'Thanks be to God'. These lines are a shortened version of a directive in accordance with Matthew 28:19 'Go into all the world and proclaim the Gospel to all Creation'. The Roman Catholic Mass liturgy attained its historically settled form by 1014 CE.

The Ordinaries and the Propers

The chants used in the Mass are classified as belonging to either the Ordinary or the Proper of the Mass. Chants of the Ordinary have texts that are invariable; the words remain the same but the musical arrangement will differ. Chants of the Proper have variable texts that are appropriate to the season of the liturgical year or of the feast day being celebrated. The Ordinary, with its unchanging texts, forms the core of the Mass liturgy, around which are placed the Scriptural readings, Psalm settings and other texts which are appropriate or Proper to the specific religious occasion. Mass may be sung at any hour from dawn until noon and on some evenings. On Christmas Eve the Mass is sung at midnight. High Mass includes chanting by a celebrant, a deacon and a sub-deacon and singing by choir, soloists and

congregation. In a Low Mass, the whole service is said or recited by one priest, with no music being sung or chanted.

Chants of the Proper

Kyrie, Gloria, Credo, Sanctus, Agnus Dei, Sequence, Tract

Chants of the Ordinary

Introit, Gradual, Alleluia, Offertario, Communio, Dismissal

Introit

The Mass begins with the Introit. This is the music accompanying the procession from its entrance into the church and up to the altar. Originally, the Introit consisted of an antiphon, a complete Psalm, the lesser Doxology (i.e. Gloria Patris) and a repetition of the antiphon. The music was sung antiphonally by two choirs – Cantai and Decani – placed on left and right of the altar. During the early ninth century CE the Introit was reduced and was performed after the celebrant reached the foot of the altar making the Introit a prelude to the service, rather than processional or entrance music. An Introit is known by the first word of its antiphon's text. For example, 'Puer Natus Est Nobis' is used for Midnight Mass at Christmas and 'Resurexi' for the Easter Mass.

Kyrie

The Introit is followed by the 'Kyrie eleison' ('Lord have mercy') and 'Agnus Dei' ('Lamb of God'). These were brought over from the Eastern Byzantine church. The Kyrie appeared in Milan in the fourth century CE and was in use in Rome by the sixth century. The Kyrie was in fact used in pre-Christian Greek pagan rites with the Christian church adding 'Christi eleison' ('Christ have mercy'). Kyrie Eleison is chanted three times, Christi eleison is chanted three times and Kyrie Eleison is chanted three times again.

Agnus Dei

The Agnus Dei was introduced in the late seventh century CE and like the Kyrie, the Agnus Dei is a petition for mercy. Originally in the chant there was only one line of text 'Agnus Dei, qui tollis peccata mundi miserere nobis' ('Lamb of God who takes away the sins of the world, have mercy on us'). Like the Sanctus this was originally sung by the congregation and over time was transferred to the choir. This chant was sung at the breaking of the bread.

Gloria

The Kyrie is followed by the Gloria, whose opening lines are the song of the heavenly host on the night of the

Nativity (Luke 2:14) and is sometimes called 'The Song of the Angels' or 'The Greater Doxology'. The Gloria is excluded on penitential days during Advent and Lent as well as from Requiem Masses. During the rite, the opening phrase 'Gloria in Excelsis Deo' ('Glory to God in the highest') is chanted by the priest and then taken up by the full choir. The Gradual follows the first reading from the Scriptures and is performed by a soloist and then the choir responds, another solo verse is sung which is repeated by the choir. The Easter Gradual is called 'Haec dies' and the Gradual for Midnight Mass is 'Viderunt omnes'.

The Alleluia

The Alleluia is an import from the Hebrew synagogue; the word means 'praise to Jehovah'. In the modern liturgy, from Easter to Pentecost the Alleluia is sung at the end of every important chant in the Proper in both Offices and Mass but is excluded from service during the penitential seasons. The Alleluia is one of the most melodious and artistic chants of the Mass.

The Tract

The Tract is called the 'Cantus Tractus' because the chant was designed to be sung from beginning to end without interruption. The Tract consists of a series of

Psalm verses performed by a soloist. This also has its roots in Hebrew synagogue solo Psalmody.

The Credo

The Credo was first used liturgically as an individual's profession of faith made to the priest at baptism. In Eastern churches this Nicene Creed was first used in the sixth century CE but it was not to be used in Gallic or Roman churches until the ninth century. With Charlemagne's reforms, the Council of Aix-la-Chapelle decreed that the Credo should be sung between the Gospel reading and Communion. However, the Credo did not officially enter the Roman Mass until 1014 CE. The celebrant priest chants the first phase 'Credo in unum Deum' ('I believe in one God'). The choir and congregation continues with 'Patrem omnipotentem' ('the Almighty Father').

The Offertory

The Offertory was introduced into the liturgy by St Augustine. The Offertory is chanted whilst the gifts of bread and wine are brought forward to be consecrated. In the early manuscripts, the Offertory consists of an antiphon, two or three verses and then a response or refrain. In the Gregorian liturgy only the antiphon remains but in the Ambrosian and Mozarabic liturgies

Offertory verses are still present. The first phrase of the Offertory is sung by the soloist and the remainder of the antiphony is performed by the choir.

Communion

The singing of a Psalm or a hymn during the Communion derives from the early Christian Church rite. In the Byzantine and Celtic rites both hymns and Psalms were used during Communion. In the Ambrosian rite two antiphons were sung and in the Roman ritual the chant consisted of an antiphon and a Psalm. Originally in the Roman church the Introit and Communion were the same Psalm but featured different antiphons. During the eleventh century Psalm verses were gradually deleted from the Communion and a century later on the antiphon remained.

Sanctus and Benedictus

This chanted acclamation combined portions of verses from both the Old and the New Testaments. The Sanctus is taken from Isaiah 6:3 and the Hosannah and Benedictus from Matthew 21:9. Originally both congregation and clergy sang the Sanctus together but eventually the transference of chanting from the whole congregation to a specialist choir happened in the eighth century CE and by the thirteenth century it was only the choir that sang the Sanctus. In the Mass there is a pause after the Sanctus, during which time the elevation of the Host occurs and then the Benedictus is sung.

The Dismissal

'Ite missa est' has always been chanted by the celebrant priest. Originally the congregation responded with 'Deo gratias' until the choir took over the full response. In the eleventh century CE an alternative dismissal chant came into use and this was 'Benedicamus Domino' ('Let us Bless the Lord').

As can be seen from the above, the modern Christian liturgy has evolved and changed considerably over centuries of use. Much of it stems from very ancient usage in pre-Christian times. It is important here to understand that these chants do not exist in isolation but as part of the Roman Mass

First Communion at a Roman church.

Painting undated by Pio Joris (1843–1921). Oil on canvas, 89 x 116 cm.

The Roman Mass in Latin

'In nomine Patris, et Filii, et Spiritus Sancti. Amen.'

Introibo ad altare Dei.

'Ad Deum qui laetificat juventutem meam.

Judica me, Deus, et discerne causam meam de gente non sancta: ab homine iniquo et doloso erue me.

Quia tu es, Deus, fortitudo mea: quare me repulisti, et quare tristis incedo, dum affligit me inimicus?

Emitte lucem tuam et veritatem tuam: ipsa me deduxerunt et adduxerunt in montem sanctum tuum, et in tabernacula tua.

Et introibo ad altare Dei: ad Deum qui laetificat juventutem meam.

Confitebor tibi in cithara, Deus, Deus meus: quare tristis es anima mea, et quare conturbas me?

Spera in Deo, quoniam adhuc confitebor illi: salutare vultus mei, et Deus meus.

Gloria Patri, et Filio, et Spiritui Sancto.

Sicut erat in principio, et nunc, et semper: et in saecula saeculorum. Amen.

Introibo ad altare Dei.

Ad Deum qui laetificat juventutem meam.

Adjutorium nostrum in nomine Domini.

Qui fecit coelum et terram.'

Confiteor

'Confiteor Deo omnipotenti, beatae Mariae semper Virgini, beato Michaeli Archangelo, beato Joanni Baptistae, sanctis Apostolis Petro et Paulo, omnibus Sanctis, et vobis, fratres, quia peccavi nimis cogitatione verbo, et opere: mea culpa, mea culpa, mea maxima culpa. Ideo precor beatam Mariam semper Virginem, beatum Michaelem Archangelum, beatum Joannem Baptistam, sanctos Apostolos Petrum et Paulum, omnes Sanctos, et vos fratres, orare pro me ad Dominum Deum Nostrum.

Misereatur tui omnipotens Deus, et dimissis peccatis tuis, perducat te ad vitam aeternam.

Amen.

Confiteor Deo omnipotenti, beatae Mariae semper Virgini, beato Michaeli Archangelo, beato Joanni Baptistae, sanctis Apostolis Petro et Paulo, omnibus Sanctis, et tibi pater: quia peccavi nimis cogitatione verbo, et opere: mea culpa, mea culpa, mea maxima culpa. Ideo precor beatam Mariam semper Virginem, beatum Michaelem Archangelum, beatum Joannem Baptistam, sanctos Apostolos Petrum et Paulum, omnes Sanctos, et te pater, orare pro me ad Dominum Deum Nostrum.

Indulgentiam, absolutionem, et remissionem peccatorum nostrorum, tributat nobis omnipotens et misericors Dominus.

Amen.

Deus, tu conversus vivificabis nos.

Et plebs tua laetabitur in te.

Ostende nobis Domine, misericordiam tuam.

Et salutare tuum da nobis.

Domine, exuadi orationem meam.

Et clamor meus ad te veniat.

Dominus vobiscum.

Et cum spiritu tuo.

Oremus.

Aufer a nobis, quaesumus, Domine, iniquitates nostras: ut ad Sancta sanctorum puris mereamur mentibus introire. Per Christum Dominum nostrum. Amen.

Oramus te. Domine, per merita Sanctorum tuorum, quorum reliquiae hic sunt, et omnium Sanctorum: ut indulgere digneris omnia peccata mea. Amen.'

Introit Antiphon

'Kyrie

Kyrie eleison.

Kyrie eleison.

Kyrie eleison.

Christe eleison.

Christe eleison.

Christe eleison.

Kyrie eleison.

Kyrie eleison.

Kyrie eleison.'

Gloria

'Gloria in excelsis Deo. Et in terra pax hominibus bonae voluntatis. Laudamus te. Benedicimus te. Adoramus te. Glorificamus te. Gratiam agimus tibi propter magnam gloriam tuam. Domine Deus, Rex coelestis, Deus Pater omnipotens. Domine Fili unigenite, Jesu Christe. Domine Deus, Agnus Dei, Filius Patris. Qui tollis peccata mundi, miserere nobis. Qui tollis peccata mundi, suscipe deprecationem nostram. Qui sedes ad dexteram Patris, miserere nobis. Quoniam tu solus Sanctus. Tu solus Dominus. To solus Altissimus, Jesu Christe. Cum Sancto Spiritu in gloria Dei Patris. Amen.

Dominus Vobiscum.

Et cum spiritu tuo.

Oremus.'

Prayer

'Per omnia saecula saeculorum.

Amen.'

Epistle

'Deo gratias.'

Gradual

'Munda cor meum

Munda cor meum ac labia mea, omnipotens Deus, qui labia Isaiae Prophetae calculo mundasti ignito: ita me tua grata miseratione dignare mundare, ut sanctum Evangelium tuum digne valeam nuntiare. Per Christum Dominum nostrum.

Amen.

Jube, Domine benedicere.

Dominus sit in corde meo et in labiis meis: ut digne et competenter annuntiem evangelium suum. Amen.'

Gospel

'Dominus vobiscum.

Et cum spiritu tuo.

Sequentia/Initium sancti Evangelii secundum N.

Gloria tibi, Domine.

Laus tibi, Christe.

Per evangelica dicta deleantur nostra delicta.'

Sermon

Nicene Creed

'Credo in unum Deum, Patrem omnipotentem, factorem coeli et terrae, visibilium omnium, et invisibilium. Et in unum Dominum Jesum Christum, Filium Dei unigenitum. Et ex Patre natum ante omnia saecula. Deum de Deo, lumen de lumine, Deum verum de Deo vero. Genitum, not factum, consubstantialem Patri: per quem omnia facta sunt. Qui propter nos homines, et propter nostram salutem descendit de coelis.

ET INCARNATUS EST DE SPIRITU SANCTO EX MARIA VIRGINE: ET HOMO FACTUS EST.

Crucifixus etiam pro nobis, sub Pontio Pilato passus, et sepultus est. Et resurrexit tertia die, secundum Scripturas. Et ascendit in coelum: sedet ad desteram Patris. Et iterum venturus est com gloria, judicare vivos et mortuos: cujus regni non erit finis. Et in Spiritum Sanctum, Dominum et vivificantem: qui ex Patre Filioque procedit. Qui cum Patre et Filio simul adoratur et conglorificatur: qui locutus est per prophetas. Et unam, sanctam, catholicam et apostolicam Ecclesiam. Confiteor unum baptisma in remissionem peccatorum. Et exspecto resurrectionem mortuorum. Et vitam ventura saeculi. Amen.

Dominus vobiscum.

Et cum spiritu tuo.

Oremus.'

Offertory

'Suscipe, sancte Pater, omnipotens aeterne Deus, hanc immaculatam hostiam, quam ego indignus

106

famulus tuus offero tibi, Deo meo vivo et vero,

pro innumerabilibus peccatis, et offensionibus,

et negligentiis meis, et pro omnibus circumstantibus,

sed et pro omnibus fidelibus Christianis vivis atque

defunctis: ut mihi, et illis proficiat ad salutem in

vitam aeternam. Amen.

Deus, qui humanae substantiae dignitatem

mirabiliter condidisti, et mirabilius reformasti:

da nobis per hujus aquae et vini mysterium, ejus

divinitatis esse consortes, qui humanitatis nostrae

fieri dignatus est particeps, Jesus Christus Filius tuus

Dominus noster: Qui tecum vivit et regnat in unitate

Spiritus Sancti Deus: per omnia saecula saeculorum.

Amen.

Offerimus tibi, Domine, calicem salutaris, tuam

deprecantes clementiam: ut in conspectu divinae

majestatis tuae, pro nostra et totius mundi salute

cum odore suavitatis ascendat.

Amen.

In spiritu humilitatis, et in animo contrito

suscipiamur a te, Domine: et sic fiat sacrificum

nostrum in conspectu tuo hodie, ut placeat tibi,

Domine Deus.

Veni, Sanctificator omnipotens aeterne Deus, et bene

dic hoc sacrificium tuo sancto nomini praeparatum.

Lavabo inter innocentes manus meas: et circumdabo

altare tuum, Domine. Ut audiam vocem laudis:

et enarrem universa mirabila tua. Domine, dilexi

decorem domus tuae: et locum habitationis gloriae

tuae. Ne perdas cum impiis, Deus animam meam:

et cum viris sanguinum vitam meam. In quorum

manibus iniquitates sunt: dextera eorum repleta est

muneribus. Ego autem in innocentia mea ingressus

sum: redime me, et miserere mei. Pes meus stetit in

directo: in ecclesiis benedicam te, Domine. Gloria

Patri, et Filio, et Spiritui Sancto. Sicut erat in

principio, et nunc, et semper: et in saecula

saeculorum. Amen.

Suscipe, sancta Trinitas, hanc oblationem, quam tibi

offerimus ob memoriam passionis, resurrectionis,

et ascensionis Jesu Christi Domini nostri: et in

honorem beatae Mariae semper Virginis, et beati

Joannis Baptistae, et sanctorum Apostolorum Petri

et Pauli, et istorum, et omnium Sanctorum: ut illis

proficiat ad honorem, nobis autem ad salutem: et illi

pro nobis intercedere dignentur in coelis, quorum memoriam agimus in terris. Per eumdem Christum Dominum nostrum.

Amen.

Orate fratres, ut meum ac vestrum sacrificium acceptabile fiat apud Deum Patrem omnipotentem.

Suscipiat Dominus sacrificium de manibus tuis, ad laudem et gloriam nominis sui, ad utilitatem quoque nostram, totiusque Ecclesiae suae sanctae.'

Secret

'Per omnia saecula saeculorum.

Amen.'

Preface

'Dominus vobiscum.

Et cum spiritu tuo.

Sursum corda.

Habemus ad Dominum.

Gratias agamus Domino Deo nostro.

Dignum et justum est.

Vere dignum et justum est, aequum et salutare, nos tibi semper, et ubique gratias agere: Domine sancte, Pater omnipotens, aeterne Deus: qui cum unigenito Filio tuo, et Spiritu Sancto, unus es Deus, unus es Dominus: non in unius singularitate personae, sed in unius Trinitate substantiae. Quod enim de tua gloria, revelante te, credimus, hoc de filio tuo, hoc de Spiritu Sancto, sine differentia discretionis sentimus. Ut in confessione verae, sempiternaeque Deitatis, et in personis proprietas, et in essentia unitas, et in majestate adoretur aequalitas. Quam laudant Angeli atque Archangeli, Cherubim quoque ac Seraphim: qui non cessant clamare quotidie, una voce dicentes:'

Sanctus

'Sanctus, Sanctus, Sanctus, Dominus Deus Sabaoth. Pleni sunt coeli et terra gloria tua. Hosanna in excelsis. Benedictus qui venit in nomine Domini.

Hosanna in excelsis.'

The Canon

'TE IGITUR, *clementissime Pater, per Jesum Christum, Filium tuum, Dominum nostrum, supplices rogamus ac petimus, uti accepta habeas, et benedicas haec dona, haec munera, haec sancta sacrificia illibata, in primis quae tibi offerimus pro Ecclesia tua sancta Catholica: quam pacificare, custodire, adunare, et regere digneris toto orbe terrarum: una cum famulo tuo Papa nostro N., et Antistite nostro N., et omnibus orthodoxis, atque catholicae et apostolicae fidei cultoribus.*

Memento, Domine, famulorum famularumque tuarum N. et N. et omnium circumstantium, quorum tibi fides cognita est, et nota devotio, pro quibus tibi offerimus, vel qui tibi offerunt hoc sacrificium laudis, pro se suisque omnibus: pro redemptione animarum suarum, pro spe salutis, et incolumitatis suae: tibique reddunt vota sua aeterno Deo, vivo et vero.

Communicantes, et memoriam venerantes, in primis gloriosae semper Virginis Mariae, Genitricis Dei et

Domini nostri Jesu Christi: sed et beatorum Apostolorum ac Martyrum tuorum, Petri et Pauli, Andreae, Jacobi, Joannis, Thomae, Jacobi, Philippi, Bartholomaei, Matthaei, Simonis, et Thaddaei: Lini, Cleti, Clementis, Xysti, Cornelii, Cypriani, Laurentii, Chrysogoni, Joannis et Pauli, Cosmae et Damiani, et omnium Sanctorum tuorum; quorum meritis, precibusque concedas, ut in omnibus protectionis tuae muniamur auxilio. Per eundem Christum Dominum nostrum. Amen.

Hanc igitur oblationem servitutis nostrae, sed et cunctae familiae tuae quaesumus, Domine, ut placatus accipias: diesque nostros in tua pace disponas, atque ab aeterna damnatione nos eripi, et in electorum tuorum jubeas grege numerari. Per Christum Dominum nostrum. Amen.

Quam oblationem tu, Deus, in omnibus, quaesumus, benedictam, adscriptam, ratam, rationabilem, acceptabilemque facere digneris: ut nobis Corpus et Sanguis fiat dilectissimi Filii tui Domini nostri Jesu Christi.'

Consecration

'Qui pridie quam pateretur, accepit panem in sanctas
ac venerabiles manus suas, et elevatis oculis in
coelum ad te Deum Patrem suum omnipotentem, tibi
gratias agens, benedixit, fregit, diditque discipulis
suis, dicens: Accipite, et manducate ex hoc omnes:

HOC EST ENIM CORPUS MEUM.

Simili modo postquam coenatum est, accipiens
et hunc praeclarum Calicem in sanctas ac venerabiles
manus suas: item tibi gratias agens, benedixit,
deditque discipulis suis, dicens: Accepite,
et bibite ex eo omnes:

HIC EST ENIM CALIX SANGUINIS MEI, NOVI ET AETERNI TESTAMENTI: MYSTERIUM FIDEI, QUI PRO VOBIS ET PRO MULTIS EFFUNDETUR IN REMISSIONEM PECCATORUM.

Haec quotiescumque feceritis, in mei memoriam facietis.

Unde et memores, Domine, nos servi tui, sed et plebs
tua sancta, ejusdem Christi Filii tui Domini nostri,
tam beatae Passionis, nec non et ab inferis

Resurrectionis, sed et in coelos gloriosae
Ascensionis: offerimus praeclarae majestati tuae de
tuis donis ac datis, hostiam puram, hostiam sanctam,
hostiam immaculatam, Panem sanctum vitae
aeternae, et calicem salutis perpetuae.

Supra quae propitio ac sereno vultu respicere
digneris, et accepta habere, sicuti accepta habere
dignatus es munera pueri tui justi Abel,
et sacrificium patriarchae nostri Abrahae, et quod
tibi obtulit summus sacerdos tuus Melchisedech,
sanctum sacrificium, immaculatam hostiam.

Supplices te rogamus, omnipotens Deus, jube haec
perferri per manus sancti Angeli tui in sublime altare
tuum, in conspectu divinae majestatis tuae: ut
quotquot ex hac altaris participatione, sacrosanctum
Filii tui Corpus, et Sanguinem sumpserimus,
omni benedictione coelesti et gratia repleamur.
Per eumdem Christum Dominum nostrum. Amen.'

Commemoration of the Dead

'Memento etiam, Domine, famulorum famularumque
tuarum N. et N. qui nos praecesserunt cum signo
fidei, et dormiunt in somno pacis.

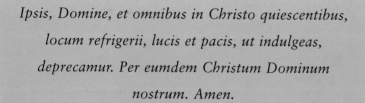

Ipsis, Domine, et omnibus in Christo quiescentibus, locum refrigerii, lucis et pacis, ut indulgeas, deprecamur. Per eumdem Christum Dominum nostrum. Amen.

Nobis quoque peccatoribus famulis tuis, de multitudine miserationum tuarum sperantibus, partem aliquam, et societatem donare digneris, cum tuis sanctis Apostolis et Martyribus: cum Joanne, Stephano, Matthia, Barnaba, Ignatio, Alexandro, Marcellino, Petro, Felicitate, Perpetua, Agatha, Lucia, Agnete, Caecilia, Anastasia, et omnibus Sanctis tuis: intra quorum nos consortium, non aestimator meriti sed veniae, quaesumus, largitor admitte. Per Christum Dominum nostrum.

Per quem haec omnia, Domine, semper bona creas, sancti ficas, vivi ficas, bene dicis, et praestas nobis.'

Minor Elevation

'Per ipsum, et cum ip so, et in ip so, est tibi Deo Patri omnipotenti, in unitate Spiritus Sancti, omnis honor et gloria. Per omnia saecula saeculorum.

Amen.'

The Communion

'Oremus. Praeceptis salutaribus moniti, et divina institutione formati, audemus dicere:

Pater noster, qui es in coelis: sanctificetur nomen tuum: adveniat regnum tuum: fiat voluntas tua, sicut in coelo, et in terra. Panem nostrum quotidianum da nobis hodie, et dimitte nobis debita nostra, sicut et nos dimittimus debitoribus nostris. Et ne nos inducas in tentationem.

Sed libera nos a malo.

Amen.

Libera nos, quaesumus, Domine, ab omnibus malis praeteritis, praesentibus, et futuris: et intercedente beata et gloriosa semper Virgine Dei Genitrice Maria, cum beatis Apostolis tuis Petro et Paulo, atque Andrea, et omnibus Sanctis, da propitius pacem in diebus nostris: ut ope misericordiae tuae adjuti, et a peccato simus semper liberi, et ab omni perturbatione securi. Per eumdem Dominum nostrum Jesum Christum Filium tuum, Qui tecum vivit et regnat in unitate Spiritus Sancti Deus.

Per omnia saecula saeculorum.

Amen.

Pax Domini sit semper vobiscum.

Et cum spiritu tuo.

Haec commixtio et consecratio Corporis et Sanguinis Domini nostri Jesu Christi, fiat accipientibus nobis in vitam aeternam. Amen.'

Agnus Dei

'Agnus Dei, qui tollis peccata mundi: miserere nobis.

Agnus Dei, qui tollis peccata mundi: miserere nobis.

Agnus Dei, qui tollis peccata mundi: dona nobis pacem.

Domine Jesu Christe, qui dixisti Apostolis tuis: Pacem relinquo vobis, pacem meam do vobis: ne respicias peccata mea, sed fidem Ecclesiae tuae:

eamque secundum voluntatem tuam, pacificare et coadunare digneris: qui vivis et regnas Deus, per omnia saecula saeculorum. Amen.

Domine Jesu Christe, Fili Dei vivi, qui ex voluntate Patris, cooperante Spiritu Sancto, per mortem tuam mundum vivificasti: libera me per hoc sacrosanctum Corpus et Sanguinem tuum ab omnibus iniquitatibus meis, et universis malis: et fac me tuis semper inhaerere mandatis, et a te numquam separari permittas. Qui cum eodem Deo Patre et Spiritu Sancto vivis et regnas Deus in saecula saeculorum. Amen.

Perceptio Corporis tui, Domine Jesu Christe, quod ego indignus sumere praesumo, non mihi proveniat in judicium et condemnationem: sed pro tua pietate prosit mihi ad tutamentum mentis et corporis, et ad medelam percipiendam: qui vivis et regnas cum Deo Patre in unitate Spiritus Sancti Deus, per omnia saecula saeculorum. Amen.'

Communion of the Priest

'Panem coelestem accipiam, et nomen Domini invocabo.

Domine, non sum dignus, ut intres sub tectum meum: sed tantum dic verbo, et sanabitur anima mea.' (repeated 3 times)

'Corpus Domini nostri Jesu Christi custodiat animam meam in vitam aeternam. Amen.'

'Quid retribuam Domino pro omnibus quae retribuit mihi? Calicem salutaris accipiam, et nomen Domini invocabo. Laudans invocabo Dominum, et ab inimicis meis salvus ero.

Sanguis Domini nostri Jesu Christi custiodiat animam meam in vitam aeternam. Amen.'

Communion of the Faithful

'Confiteor Deo omnipotenti, beatae Mariae semper Virgini, beato Michaeli Archangelo, beato Joanni Baptistae, sanctis Apostolis Petro et Paulo, omnibus Sanctis, et tibi Pater: quia peccavi nimis cogitatione verbo, et opere: mea culpa, mea culpa, mea maxima culpa. Ideo precor beatam Mariam semper Virginem, beatum Michaelem Archangelum, beatum Joannem

Baptistam, sanctos Apostolos Petrum et Paulum, omnes Sanctos, et te Pater, orare pro me ad Dominum Deum Nostrum.

Misereatur vestri omnipotens Deus, et dimissis peccatis tuis, perducat te ad vitam aeternam.

Amen.

Indulgentiam, absolutionem, et remissionem peccatorum nostrorum, tributat nobis omnipotens et misericors Dominus.

Amen.'

'Ecce Agnus Dei, ecce qui tollit peccata mundi.

Domine, non sum dignus, ut intres sub tectum meum: sed tantum dic verbo, et sanabitur anima mea.' (repeated 3 times)

'Corpus Domini nostri Jesu Christi custodiat animam tuam in vitam aeternam. Amen.'

The Ablutions

'Quod ore sumpisimus, Domine, pura mente
capiamus: et de munere temporali fiat nobis
remedium sempiternum.

Corpus tuum, Domine, quod sumpsi,
et Sanguis, quem potavi, adhaereat visceribus meis:
et praesta, ut in me non remaneat scelerum macula,
quem pura et sancta refecerunt Sacramenta:
Qui vivis et regnas in saecula saeculorum. Amen.'

Communion Prayer

'Dominus vobiscum.
Et cum spiritu tuo.
Oremus.
Postcommunion

Amen.'

French manuscript illumination, thirteenth-century mass book
of King Louis. Showing a page with music.

 # The Post-Council of Trento Gregorian Chant (1500–Present Day)

THE COUNCIL OF TRENTO

Although Charlemagne's reforms were successful in creating a common liturgical practice throughout Europe, there had never been an attempt to create uniformity or to limit the national evolution of the liturgy. Since liturgical texts were disseminated through hand-copied books throughout the monasteries, there was always an opportunity to include local adaptations and innovations each time a new manuscript was produced. Each diocese had its own liturgical calendar of feasts and its own unique way of performing certain ritual details. This evolution included the addition of the sequence to the mass which was a non-biblical song inserted after the Alleluia and in some areas a proper sequence was sung on every Sunday and major feast day. Another type of liturgical evolution was the addition of phrases of musical text referred to as Tropes. Often Tropes acted as introductions to existing chant and like the Sequences the Tropes were used on Sundays and feast days.

The major musical innovation of the Middle Ages was the development of polyphonic choral singing. At first a traditional chant was elaborated on by the addition of a second improvised vocal line. A third line might then be added, creating a new complex chant. Many of these compositions became so elaborate that the texts were no longer intelligible to the listeners. The Council of Trento was convened by Pope Paul III in Italy in 1545 CE and continued until 1563 CE under the leadership of four different Popes. The Council established a system of seminaries to improve the quality of clergy and decreed that each Bishop had to reside in his own diocese, a responsibility that was being neglected. In response to the Protestant reformers the Council of Trento affirmed the Catholic Church's traditional beliefs in the sacrificial nature of the Eucharist and in the Doctrine of the Real Presence (meaning that the bread and wine really do change). It also called for the continued use of Latin in liturgy but there was no specific condemnation of the use of the vernacular. In the matter of music, polyphonic music was permitted in addition to the use of traditional

chant as long as the texts of polyphonic pieces were not unduly obscured. At this Council the use of Tropes was banned entirely and the use of Sequences was suppressed except for a handful of favourites.

The liturgical ideas that were set forth at the Council of Trento were published by Pope Pius V in 1580 CE. The structure of the Mass remained the same general shape as it was at the time of Charlemagne and the most important effect of the Council of Trento was the intense regulation of every

used exactly as prescribed, without change or addition and that this liturgy was the definitive one. This strict uniformity was set out in the hope that the Protestant Reformation would fail to infect Catholic worship. However, in spite of this desire for extreme uniformity, the fathers of the Council of Trento permitted the continuation of the Milanese and Mozarabic rites.

liturgical detail. Unlike the hand-copied books of earlier centuries the printing press assured that all copies of the new liturgical books were exactly the same in every church. Pius V decreed that all rites and texts were to be

French book illumination from the book of hours of Jean, Duc de Berry, with script and ornament depicting priests, monks and believers celebrating the High Mass.

The types of Mass set out by Pius V at the Council of Trento were divided into three forms called Solemn, High and Low Masses. The Solemn Mass followed the traditional shape of liturgy whereby the presiding bishop or priest was assisted by one or more deacons, sub-deacons, lectors, acolytes and singers. The High Mass was performed with a single priest assisted by only a few lay servers. In the High Mass, a choir performed all the chants contained therein. In a Low Mass there was no choir and the texts of the chants were recited by the priest alone. Most congregations experienced their liturgy only in the two simpler forms. During this period, polyphonic music and the Rococo style of art changed the experience of worship. This new style of art with its vibrant colours and dramatic depictions of interior scenes filled the interiors of the churches with a highly evocative visual display. Polyphonic choral singing and the use of musical instruments alongside the organ led to the creation of large musical productions in the context of liturgy. The members of the congregation who could no longer understand the Latin texts or participate in the ritual could now watch and listen to a dramatic ritual of artistic splendour.

THE DECLINE OF THE CHANT

In the early sixteenth century the pace at which the chant was sung slowed down considerably. This was because the organum required a slower pace to ensure that the singers kept in time with one another. The first complete chant book published after the reforms of the Council of Trento presented chant in proportional notation. This notation formed a new style in itself but it was unfortunately slow and tedious. Between 1577 and 1613 CE polyphonic composers in Rome were asked to realign the chant melodies in order to fit the adjusted texts of the Council of Trento. The composers went well beyond their brief and modified the chants to make them conform to the rules of sixteenth century polyphony. These changes included removing long melismas, altering the length and number of notes per syllable, changing the cadences and adding musical patterns to represent particular words. The reformed chants were then published and accepted by the church as the official version of post-Trento Gregorian chant. In some regions during the seventeenth and eighteenth century chant itself seems to have dropped out of use altogether. In Italy and France, Baroque and operatic sacred music became popular. In Germany and Austria many congregations became

devoted to symphonic masses such as those composed by Haydn, Mozart and Beethoven. No longer were the words and therefore the chant voice important, rather the musical instrumentation and composition took over the minds, hearts and souls of the people.

Figured Chant

Figured chant, which was based on newer melodies, was elaborately ornamented by the singers as well as being accompanied by the organ. This type of chant was introduced into France alongside the eighteenth century neo-Gallican movement which also instituted many changes to the liturgy.

Counterpoint Chant

Counterpointed chant was a kind of improvised polyphony in which the standard chant melodies served as a centre around which singers extemporised. The Church itself put up with the changes to liturgical music, merely laying down principles to preclude practices that impeded the liturgy, particularly insisting that the orchestra should not dominate the voices of the choir and that the music should serve the liturgy, not vice versa.

THE CAECILIAN MOVEMENT

In Germany the Caecilian Movement was formed to improve church music, particularly in Europe and the Americas. The movement's aim was to promote the use of sixteenth century polyphony and reform the chant. The Caecilian Movement was strongly supported by the Church and in fact one of its chief members Frances Xavier Haberle (1840–1910 CE) was employed by the Church to edit a revised edition of the Medicean chantbook. In France, post-Enlightenment anti-Papal feeling was followed by a period of spiritual renewal. The Church in France adopted the Roman liturgy again and new medieval manuscripts were discovered. Scholastic studies of chanting began to appear and there were attempts made to produce new chant books based on the older ones. Unfortunately, opinion differed as to what the correct melodies and rhythms of Gregorian chant were until the work of the monks of the Abbey of Saint Pierre de Solesmes emerged from the shadows.

THE ABBEY OF SAINT PIERRE DE SOLESMES

The land containing the Abbey of Solesmes had been used for organised public worship from as early as the

fifth century CE. By the beginning of the ninth century the church of Le Mans in Solesmes was held by a vassal of Charlemagne's court. After the Norman raids the church and its surroundings fell into the hands of Raoul de Beaumont, Viscount of le Maine. He passed the ownership to his brother Geoffroy who in turn donated it to the monks of La Couture on 12th October 1010 CE which is the date that the present-day monastery of Solesmes acknowledges as its foundation. Little information is known about the monastery during the twelfth and thirteenth centuries but in 1375 CE Solesmes experienced the sufferings brought on by the interminable Hundred Years War and fifty years later the area was occupied by English invaders who burnt down the monastery. After 1425 CE the generosity of several benefactors helped bring the monastery back to life. Philibert de la Croix initiated the roof vaulting of the church around 1475 CE. From 1486 to 1495 Cheminart built a belltower and also commissioned the Tomb of our Lord sculpture located in the south transept. From 1532 CE onwards, Jean Boguler completed the vaulting of the entire church, made improvements to the sanctuaries and undertook the sculptures in the 'Belle Chapelle' in the north transept. Unfortunately, because of the Concordat of Boulogne, the King of France disposed of the Priory at Solesmes, thus depriving the monks of their religious superiors and so the house began to decline in increasing numbers and slipped into increasing decadence.

In December 1664 CE Gabriel de Chaource-Beauregard took on the Abbey of Solesme. Forty years later in 1723 CE the conventual lodgings were completely rebuilt by Jean-Baptiste Colbert, the Marquis of Torcy. Then on 13th February 1790 CE, in the wake of the French Revolution, the new French constitution outlawed religious vows and the monks of Solesmes were forced to disperse. Officially the Priory was sold off but no new owner ever came forward. On two different occasions, in 1792 and 1794 CE, the villagers saved the monastery's most prized relic, a thorn from what was believed to be the crown of thorns of Jesus. It was not until 1850 CE that the relic was returned to the monastery where it is still housed.

Prosper Guéranger

Guéranger was born in Sublé in 1805 CE. At the age of twenty-two he was ordained as a priest. He worked for the Bishop of Paris as his secretary and in 1831 CE he discovered that the Priory at Solesmes was destined for destruction for lack of a buyer. He decided to find the means to acquire it and take up a monastic Benedictine life. With the help of friends and with the support of the Bishop he was able to find the money to rent the property and moved in with three companions on 11th July 1833 CE. The buildings were run-down and the small community had no money and no experience of monastic life. Guéranger took his inspiration from solid monastic traditions, particularly that of the true spirit of St Benedict and bolstered by the Benedictine liturgy and spiritual life he became a living example of his ideals to his monks and soon the monastery attracted a list of benefactors. In 1837 CE he travelled to Rome to ask for official recognition of Solesmes as a Benedictine community. The Vatican not only granted his request but raised Solesmes from the status of priory to that of an abbey, making it the head of a new Benedictine congregation of France.

Guéranger is known above all for the part he played for the resurrection of the Latin liturgy in France. The meaning and value of the rite had long been forgotten. The return of the Dioceses of France to the Roman liturgy is owed in large measure to him. Holding the Church's chant to be the perfect expression of liturgical prayer, he undertook the restoration of the Gregorian melodies which centuries of neglect and changes in taste had left unrecognisable.

In 1853 CE, with the support of the Bishop of Le Mans, Guéranger resuscitated the ancient monastery of St Martin of Tours. In 1886 CE he founded St Cecilia's of Solesmes under the direction of Madame Cecile Bruyéré its first Abbess. Guéranger had been her spiritual mentor since her childhood. He also founded the German Benedictine congregation of Beuron. Guéranger died in January 1875 CE and his body lies in the crypt of the Abbey of Solesmes.

After Dom Guéranger's death, the monastery went through years of constant hardship and the monastery

was abandoned on numerous occasions. In 1890 CE a new Prior, named Dom Paul Delatte, decided to re-open the monastery which he duly did on 23rd August that year. A large building programme was launched and two more groups of monks left to form more foundations, one at St Michael's in Farnborough, Hampshire, England and the other was St Anne at Kergonan near Plouharmel in Brittany, France in 1897 CE. Following a number of years which allowed the community to live and grow in peace, once again French law intervened. In 1901 CE a law was passed forbidding all religious congregations and the community of Solesmes closed down and moved to the Isle of Wight off England where they established a number of communities. In 1908 CE they moved into the ancient Abbey of Quarr on the north coast of the Isle of Wight and began constructing a new monastery there.

Quarr Abbey on the Isle of Wight.

In 1922 CE the Abbot Dom Germaine Cozien led a group of monks back to Solesmes from the Isle of Wight. The First World War had allowed for more religious tolerance in France. During the Second World War and the Nazi occupation, although three of the monks were killed and many imprisoned, daily life in the monastery went on and more buildings were erected. In 1948 CE Dom Cozien and a group of monks worked to restore the old Trappist Abbey of Our Lady at Font Gombault. His successor Dom Jean Prou set up a series of monasteries and foundations in Africa. The current Abbot of Solesmes since 1992 CE is Fr Philipe Dupont and in 1997 CE he opened another monastery in Lithuania. The monastic and contemplative ideals of the first Abbot Dom Guéranger are still maintained today, both at the monastery of Solesmes itself and at the twenty-eight other monasteries which sprung out of it throughout the world. The tradition of the Gregorian chant continues to be sung each day as was originally intended. The monks of Solesmes gather the required seven times a day for prayer and produce a perpetual chant throughout the day.

The Abbey of Solesmes.

THE SECOND VATICAN COUNCIL

During the nineteenth and twentieth centuries CE scholars gained a greater understanding of the history of liturgy. Many old manuscripts were rediscovered and reinterpreted. The science of comparative liturgics emerged where the various forms of liturgy were studied. This led scholars to understand the roots of all Christian worship and this in turn promoted the desire to return to a purer, more primitive form of religious rites. Scholars have discovered that the liturgy of the Council of Trento had moved away drastically from the earlier liturgies in their eagerness to win converts. It was time for another liturgical form. During the 1950s Pope Pius XII began to replace the late medieval versions of the liturgy with older, more traditional ones. This restoration was well received at all levels. Many were also calling for more use of the vernacular language because it had been proven to be more pastorally effective in the Orthodox and the Protestant churches.

On 25th January 1959 CE, Pope John XXIII suddenly called for a General Council of the Catholic Church. In its first session in 1962 CE this Pope set a tone of extreme openness and debate and reform. A broad list of topics was discussed: three particularly important areas were the relationship of the Roman Catholic Church with other Christian churches, the increased role of the laity in the ministry and a complete reform of the liturgy. The Council's liturgical document 'Constitution of the Sacred Liturgy' was one of the first documents issued and its principles were implemented immediately. There were huge changes brought about in liturgical practice. The reform was quite explicit in that it called for changes that would allow the congregation to participate more fully in the services. The first goal was to restore a more simplified form of rite. In terms of style it called for the avoidance of repetition and long prayer texts. Although it called for a retention of Latin as a language of worship it also recommended the use of the vernacular languages which would apply not just to the text of the liturgy but to the chants. The Constitution gave a greater flexibility to the creation of variations and adaptations of various ritual elements. These changes in the liturgy were published in a Missal of Paul VI in 1969 CE. The new rite reinstated the use of the traditional liturgical books: The Sacramentary, The Lectionary and Chant Books.

The Mass of Paul VI restored one ancient element that had been missing since the time of Gregory I, namely the intercessory prayers concluding the Liturgy of the Word described by Justin Martyr in 150 CE. The model forms of this intercession are more in the style of the Byzantine

litany form. The new Missal also included a number of new Eucharistic prayers and the Communion and concluding rites retained the same form that was used in the time of Gregory I. The Constitution of the Sacred Liturgy recommends the continued use of Gregorian chant whilst admitting other musical styles. The Missal of Paul VI gives the option of using all the traditional Gregorian Proper chants but allows for very general alternatives. The Missal also gives a greater flexibility and allows for very many options determined by the local church or presiding minister. While some communities celebrate the liturgy using tradition Gregorian repertoire, very many modern parishes use a variety of songs from the secular stage, which although currently popular with the congregation would seem to have little lasting merit and often have little connection with any liturgical tradition.

'The Gregorian Mass'. Pope Gregory I celebrates Mass.

Taken from a Book of Hours.

Pope John XXIII

Angelo Roncalli was born into a family of farmers in November 1881 CE in Northern Italy. At the age of twelve he entered the seminary at Bergamo and then went to Rome. His education was interrupted when he served for a year as a volunteer in the Italian army. He returned to the seminary to take a doctorate in Theology and was ordained in August 1904. He was then appointed as secretary to the new Bishop of Bergamo, as well as teaching at his own seminary. In 1915 he was recalled to the army and served in the Medical and Chaplaincy Corp. After the First World War he was made the spiritual director of the seminary at Bergamo. In 1921 he was called to Rome and made Director of the Society for the Propagation of the Faith in Italy. He was consecrated Archbishop in 1925 and sent to Bulgaria. In 1934 he visited Turkey and Greece and met with the Ecumenical Patriarch Benjamin in 1939. During the Second World War Istanbul became a centre for espionage and the Archbishop assisted the escape of a number of Jews from persecution from the Nazis.

Pope John XXIII, 1962.

When he was sixty-four years old he was sent to Paris as Nuncio (Papal Ambassador), where he worked to help smooth over the divisions caused by the war. At the age of seventy-two he was made Cardinal and Patriarch of Venice and this was the first time he had charge of a large diocese. When he was seventy-seven he was elected Pope upon the death of Pius XIII. During his short time as Pope he expanded and internationalised the College of Cardinals, called the first Diocesan Synod of Rome in history, revised the Code of Canon Law and called the Second Vatican Council to revitalise the Church with the ultimate goal of the reunification of all Christian churches. This Council marked the beginning of a new spirit of openness on the part of Rome towards Christians not of the Papal obedience. There is a story told that when it was announced that Protestant leaders would be invited to the Council as observers, the conservative Cardinal Ottaviani was horrified and said to Pope John XXIII 'Your Holiness, Protestants are heretics'. The Pope responded by saying 'Not heretics, my son, say separated brethren'. 'But they are in league with the Devil, Your Holiness' replied the Cardinal. 'Do not say Devil, my Son, say separated Angel' insisted the Pope.

This small story demonstrates the tolerance, openness, intelligence and love of his fellow humans that Pope

John XXIII was renowned for. He died on 3rd June 1963 CE having won the widespread affection of both Christians and non-Christians alike.

Mass at St Peter's Square with Pope Paul VI during the second Vatican Council, 1965.

The Modern Greek and Russian Orthodox Chant

In the latter part of the nineteenth century, a search was undertaken in order to free Russian liturgical music from foreign influences. The Moscow Synodal School attempted to establish a new direction for church music by returning to the early Russian Church Unison melodies and using those melodies for composing church music, rather than using Gregorian Chant as their basis.

Prior to the Bolshevik Revolution the Russian theological schools in their studies of historical liturgyology laid the groundwork for the evaluation of Orthodox worship. During a very short period, from the 1880s to 1917, a vast repertoire of Russian church compositions was created. Composers such as Tchaikovsky, Rimski-Korsakov and Rachmaninov wrote church music using the old Russian chants as thematic material. Since the Berlin Wall has come down Russia has begun a renaissance in the spiritual lives of its people. Whereas during Communism the orthodox churches of Russia were forced to meet in secret and many priests and devotees were persecuted and murdered by the regime, a religious freedom has opened up. With it a new appreciation of the Eastern Orthodox liturgy and the beauty of its music has come about. As of yet little of it has filtered through to the West but with the coming of the World Wide Web and the international recording industry the glories of the Eastern Orthodox chant will be celebrated once again throughout the world.

The Protestant and Anglican Chant

Protestantism has a myriad of contemporary forms and is mostly known for not being liturgical. Only the Anglican Church of England is liturgical in the historic sense of the term. Why should this be?

The Protestant reformers made conscious choices in the area of liturgics and liturgical music, as much as they did in theology and doctrine. Liturgical music did not develop for purely aesthetic purposes. Rather it evolved within the Judeao-Christian traditions as both a central part of the worship experience and as a means of intensifying and beatifying that experience. The experience centred around a universal event, i.e. the Eucharist. Orthodox liturgy and the Roman Mass, although containing other elements, can mostly be traced back to the structure of the Jewish synagogue service. This sacramental orientation is fundamental to the liturgical nature of Christianity. The Protestant reformers attempted to refute sacrementality.

Russian Patriarch of Moscow and All Russia, Alexiy II, leads the night Christmas service at the Christ the Saviour Cathedral in Moscow, January, 2002. Russian Orthodox believers celebrate Christmas by the Julian calendar, which runs two weeks behind the Gregorian calendar.

Many Protestant denominations rejected liturgical worship along with the sacraments and began adopting a different approach. The contrast between the Roman Mass held in a cathedral and a Quaker meeting is enormous. The Puritans deplore all outer forms of worship and their hierarchies and have a more personal and simplified way of worshipping their God. Their way is, in fact, closer to the way of Islam. This may seem like a theological dichotomy when both denominations believe and worship in a God of the same name. The English Puritans' crusade against all forms of sensuous beauty in worship has had a profound effect upon our notion of worship in the Western world. The Protestant Puritan working hypothesis was also well put by the Roman poet Perseus or the pagan philosopher Seneca in the first century and these in turn are only elaborating a thesis from Greek philosophical authors going back to the seventh century BCE.

Briefly, the Protestant Puritan theory is that worship is a purely mental activity to be exercised by a strictly psychological focus to a subjective emotional experience. All external things which might impair this fixed focus of attention must be removed. Unfortunately, the mind itself is full of distracting pictures and the Puritan mind tends to descend into depths of despair and self-loathing that the Roman Catholic would have no experience of. The principal defect of Protestant Puritanism is its tendency to verbalise, to believe that words alone can express or stimulate the act of worship. They had difficulty moving beyond the first verse of their Bible, i.e. 'In the beginning was the Word ...'. Because of their inability to associate the joys of life with the worship of God, they had not developed a musical tradition in the way that Roman Catholicism or the Eastern Orthodox Churches had.

However, the Anglican Church continues in their services to emulate a form of the Roman Catholic Mass, albeit sung and spoken in the English vernacular. The Anglican liturgy and chant closer resembles that of the original Celtic Christian traditions of the British Isles. They celebrate a variant of the High Mass. The Anglican Church was at its peak during the Victorian era (1837–1901 CE). Many of the mock-Gothic churches seen in the cities and countryside of the British Isles, and other associated provinces, date back to that period. The yearly liturgical calendar and the choral singing is unique in itself.

Nearly all Psalm settings used in collegiate churches and cathedrals from the time of the first English Prayer Book

in 1550 until the English Civil War and the temporary suppression of Anglican liturgy, were harmonised Plainchant. In Parish churches the liturgy was usually spoken; singing would be metrical Psalmody and it was usually extra-liturgical. All adapted Plainchant melodies reflect the fact that during the period when they were made, the Latin chant itself was undergoing a process of simplification. The chant was altered so that accented syllables received more or longer notes than unaccented ones. The chant was performed more slowly and the notation recorded a binary rhythmic relation between long and short notes, thereby producing rhythmic configurations similar to modern-day musical notation of crotchets and quavers.

During the time of the Restoration the tradition was interrupted and there was a great need for instruction books in liturgical music. It was then that composers began to write new Anglican chants, the performance of which was strongly influenced by the same rhythmic performance style. This continued until the twentieth century when equalist rhythm was adopted in the wake of the influence of the monks of Solesmes. At this time the Oxford Movement revived the belief that the Eucharist should be the main focus of Christian worship. This led to a revival of singing at the Eucharist in the Anglican Church for the first time since the Reformation. This paved the way for the revival of the Gregorian chants for the Mass as well as for the Divine Office. In many parts of the Anglican Church it became customary to use an English translation of the Roman Missal in preference to the Rite of the Book of Common Prayer. The use of chant has been controversial in the Catholic Church only since the Second Vatican Council. The modern chant revival in the Church of England has been controversial because of its association in the minds of Protestants with Roman Catholicism ('Popery'). However, more recently there has been a greater flexibility and tolerance towards its use. The Royal School of Church Music has helped to bring the Gregorian chant to a wider cross-section of people including choirs from the free churches and an ecumenical atmosphere prevails once again.

The English interest and participation in polyphony are attested by surviving manuscripts, particularly the Old Hall manuscript and the second Winchester Troper. In Britain the most active centres of polyphony were the Benedictine abbeys. The old St Andrew's Manuscript was compiled for and used in the Augustinian priory of St Andrew's, Scotland. It contains a repertory of Ordinary and Proper sections for a cycle of Votive Masses of the Blessed Virgin Mary. The music is mainly two-part polyphony in descant style. The Manuscript comes from the middle of the thirteenth century.

The performance of polyphonic music in the liturgy is specifically detailed in some of the 'Customaries of the Use of Sarum'. For example, on Christmas Day and the following four days the Benedicamus was to be sung in two-part polyphony. At Westminster Abbey and St Augustine's in Canterbury the Benedictus, Magnificat, Sequences and some Processionals were sung in two-part polyphony on principal feast days. Only partial manuscripts of English liturgical music from the middle and late fifteenth century are extant. The Eton College Choirbook has polyphonic votive antiphons honouring the Virgin Mary as well as settings for the Magnificat. The Egerton Manuscript has a repertory of Sarum liturgical music, as well as some carols. The harmonies reflect the English preference for hexachords.

CHANT BOOKS

What follows is a list of books deemed to be essential for the performance of Gregorian chant.

Chant Books for the Mass in Latin

'Graduale Romanum' (1974), 'Graduale Triplex' (1979), 'Offertoriale Triplex' (1985), 'Graduale Simplex' (Libreria Editrici Vaticani), The Gregorian Missal, Liber Cantulais.

Chant Books for the Divine Office in Latin

Liber Responsorialis, Nocturnale Romanum, Antiphonale Monasticum, Psalterium Monasticum (1981), Antiphonal Romanum Secundum Liturgiam Horarum Tomus Alter: Liber Hymnarius (1983), Liber Cantualis (1978).

Many Protestant denominations rejected liturgical worship along
with the sacraments and began adopting a different approach.
The contrast between the Roman Mass held in a cathedral and
a Quaker meeting is enormous.

 # Epilogue: The Chant in other Religious Traditions

In the past four chapters we have traced the history of religious chanting from Ancient Egypt to the present day. However, the religious chant has a tradition amongst all peoples of the world and is not solely confined to the beliefs of Judaeo-Christianity. Various scientific studies have also shown how the effects of sound can produce altered states of consciousness and mystical visions.

HINDU CHANTING

In India the chant is called a mantra and it is either used as an invocation or an evocation. A mantra contains a sacred syllable or a set of syllables and when uttered with specified rhythms with phonetic and grammatical accuracy that are prescribed by the spiritual injunctions of the Vedas (the sacred texts pertaining to Hinduism) it is believed to compel the deity to assist the invoker to achieve the desired end. The mantras and chants are also used in order to praise the deities but always by way of propitiation. For example, Lakshmi 'Om Sri Maha Lakshmyai Namah'.

According to Hindu beliefs if a mantra or chant is pronounced correctly the deity to whom it is addressed has no choice but to respond. When a complicated ritual performed by groups of priests chanting various mantras is held, not one but many deities are invoked simultaneously. The chanting creates the necessary vibrations in the atmosphere to awaken the deities and facilitate their descent into the place of worship. It is believed that hidden in each mantra is the energy of a particular deity which remains normally latent and then becomes active the moment the mantra is pronounced.

The exterior view of a Hindu temple at Siolem in Goa, India.

125

BUDDHIST CHANT

Like Hindus the Buddhists practice mantra recitation but because Buddhism is more of a cross-cultural religion than Hinduism, the Tibetan Buddhist chant is quite different from the Japanese Buddhist chant. The most widely used mantra in Tibetan Buddhism is 'Om Mani Padme Hum' which means 'Praise the Jewel in the Lotus Flower'. In Zen Buddhism practitioners chant the Heart Sutra which ends with the mantra 'Gate Gate Paragate Parasamgate Bodhi Svaha!' which means 'Gone, Gone, gone beyond, gone beyond beyond, awakening, give praise!'. This mantra is most usually sounded within the mind during meditation. Another sect of Buddhism called Nicheren uses the 'Namu Myoho Renge Kyo' mantra which means 'Homage to the Lotus Sutra'.

Amoghasiddhi, one of the five transcendental buddhas, West Tibet. Gouache on canvas, end of fourteenth, beginning of fifteenth century.

ISLAMIC CHANT

In the Koran it says 'Oh ye mountains! Sing ye back the praises of God with him.' (Surah 34, Verse 10). While the Koran mentions God's praises being sung by David and even by angels, it makes no mention of singing as an act of congregational worship. This stands out in contrast to the congregational singing of sacred songs in the Hebrew Bible. Another striking contrast is seen in the Islamic rule against singing with musical accompaniment in the mosque. What is unusual is that both the Bible and the Koran teach that the Holy Men of the past, such as David, praised God with both songs and instruments in the Temple. The Koran does not mention singing in joyful response to God's salvation. However, tradition says that memorising all ninety-nine names of Allah, from the Compassionate to the Patient, ensures entry to Paradise for the faithful. These are normally memorised in the form of chant.

Islamic ornamental tile with inscription 'Allah is great'.
Turkish, nineteenth-century.

NORTH AMERICAN NATIVE CHANTING

'The first woman holds it in her hands, she holds the moon in her hands, in the centre of the sky she holds it in her hands, as she holds it in her hands it starts upwards'. The Navaho are the second largest Indian tribe in the United States. Their 60 million acre reservation includes parts of Arizona, New Mexico and Utah. For the Navaho chanting is a celebration of life, harmony and healing and their sacred songs have kept their culture alive. With mythology and ritual the medicine men and women chant to help heal the sick, prevent illness and protect people from evil.

'Before me peaceful, behind me peaceful, under me peaceful, over me peaceful, all around me peaceful.'

Navaho Indians Tonenili, Tobadzischini and Nayenezgani, in ceremonial dress for the Yebichai ceremony.
Photograph by Edward S. Curtis, 1904/05.

THE GREGORIAN CHANT REVIVAL

In the last decade of the twentieth century a very unusual phenomenon occurred when what had been a form of religious music became popular in a mainstream secular way. It was an EMI record executive who was on a holiday in Spain and who had come across an obscure collection of Gregorian chant recordings that initiated the Gregorian chant revival. EMI were persuaded to purchase the rights of a small independent Spanish label's Gregorian chants that had been recorded in the early 1970s by a group of cloistered Benedictine monks. The monastery of Santo Domingo de Silos until then had remained obscure to the world outside, only visited by pilgrims stopping on their way to Santiago de Compostella; now its inhabitants were to become world famous for their chanting. The record company utilised a powerful advertising and marketing strategy to ensure that the record-buying public and in particular their target of young people would be enchanted by the sound of Gregorian chant. At first 'Canto Gregoriano', as the album was called, was only sold in Spain to test its appeal. Within a few months it had sold in the hundreds of thousands and so it was decided to release it on a pan-global scale. It sold into the millions becoming a Top Ten album in almost every country it was available in. A follow-up album 'Chant' was also released and this too became a best-seller. Since then more recordings by other choirs have meant a flood of Gregorian chant albums can be found in people's CD players in cars and living rooms everywhere.

The Roman Catholic Church liturgy today, although following in essence the traditional rite, can be experienced in a wide context of performance. One can visit a monastery and experience the Mass as it was performed in the seventh century, a cathedral that may use the medieval styles or a modern Catholic church where rock n' roll accompanies the minister. Many modern dance records are also incorporating the Gregorian chant and the New Age movement has readily adopted it for the purpose of meditation, regardless of a belief in the Christian God or not.

> *'Glória in excélsis Deo Et in térrapax homínibus bónæ voluntátis.'*
>
> *'Glory to God in the highest, and on earth peace to men of good will.'*

 # Index